Honda C50, C70 & C90

Service and Repair Manual

by Mervyn Bleach and Jeremy Churchill

(324 - 9AE15 - 176)

Models covered

C50	49cc	Feb '67 to Jul '77
C50Z-2	49cc	May '77 to May '79
C50Z-Z	49cc	May '79 to Mar '83
C50Z-A (C50L)	49cc	Mar '80 to Jun '83
C50-C	49cc	Feb '82 to Jul '84
C50-E	49cc	Feb '84 to Apr '85
C70	72cc	Feb '72 to Jul '77
C70Z-2	72cc	May '77 to Jul '79
C70Z-Z	72cc	Jul '79 to Mar '83
C70-C	72cc	Mar '82 to Jul '84
C70-E	72cc	Aug '84 to Mar '86
C90 (C90)	89cc	Sept '67 to Jul '77
C90Z-2	89cc	May '77 to May '79
C90 Z-Z	89cc	May '79 to Aug '83
C90-C	89cc	Mar '83 to Feb '84
C90-E	89cc	Feb '84 to Sept '86
C90-G	89cc	Sept '86 to Apr '92
C90-N	89cc	May '92 to Sept '93
C90-P	89cc	Sept '93 to May '96
C90-T	89cc	May '96 to Jan '03
C90M-F	86cc	Apr '85 to Sept '86
C90M-G	86cc	Sept '86 to Apr '93
C90M-N	86cc	Dec '92 to Sept '93
C90M-P	86cc	Sept '93 to May '96
C90M-T	86cc	May '96 to Jan '03

Note: The C50LA automatic transmission models are not covered in this manual.

© Haynes Publishing 2006

A book in the Haynes Service and Repair Manual Series

ABCDE
FGHIJ
KLM
2

Printed in the USA

Haynes Publishing
Sparkford, Yeovil, Somerset BA22 7JJ, England

Haynes North America, Inc
861 Lawrence Drive, Newbury Park, California 91320, USA

Editions Haynes
4, Rue de l'Abreuvoir
92415 COURBEVOIE CEDEX, France

Haynes Publishing Nordiska AB
Box 1504, 751 45 UPPSALA, Sweden

ISBN 1 84425 375 9

British Library Cataloguing in Publication Data
A catalogue record for this book is available from the British Library.

About this manual

The author of this manual has the conviction that the only way in which a meaningful and easy to follow text can be written is first to do the work himself, under conditions similar to those found in the average household. As a result, the hands seen in the photographs are those of the author. Even the machine was not new: an example that had covered a considerable mileage was selected so that the conditions encountered would be typical of those found by the average owner. Unless specially mentioned, and therefore considered essential, Honda service tools have not been used. There is invariably some alternative means of loosening a vital component when service tools are not available but risk of damage should always be avoided.

Each of the eight Chapters is divided into numbered Sections. Within these Sections are numbered paragraphs. Cross reference throughout the manual is quite straightforward and logical. When reference is made 'See Section 6.10', it means Section 6, paragraph 10 in the same Chapter. If another Chapter were meant, the reference would read 'See Chapter 2, Section 6.10'.

All paragraphs are captioned with a Section/paragraph number to which they refer, and are relevant to the Chapter text adjacent. Figures (usually line illustrations) appear in a logical but numerical order, within a given Chapter. Fig. 1.1. therefore refers to the first figure in Chapter 1.

Left-hand and right-hand descriptions of the machines and their components refer to the left and right of a given machine when the rider is seated normally.

Motorcycle manufacturers continually make changes to specifications and recommendations, and these, when notified, are incorporated into our manuals at the earliest opportunity.

We take great pride in the accuracy of information given in this manual, but motorcycle manufacturers make alterations and design changes during the production run of a particular motorcycle of which they do not inform us. No liability can be accepted by the authors or publishers for loss, damage or injury caused by any errors in, or omissions from, the information given.

Acknowledgements

Thanks are due to Fran Ridewood and Co of Wells, Somerset, for supplying the C70 model featured in the main text of this manual and to Honda (UK) Limited for the technical assistance given during the preparation of this manual.

Paul and Chris Branson of Paul Branson Motorcycles of Yeovil, supplied the models featured in the update Chapter and the C90 shown on the front cover.

Thanks are also due to the Avon Rubber Company who kindly supplied information and technical assistance on tyre fitting; NGK Spark Plugs (UK) Limited who supplied information on sparking plug maintenance and electrode conditions; and Renold Limited who gave advice on chain care and renewal.

Contents

1977 Honda C50 model

1977 Honda C90 model

Introduction to the Honda 50, 70 and 90 models

During February 1967 Honda, already well known for their step-through scooter style machine, introduced into the UK their overhead camshaft engine version of the 50 cc motorcycle.

This technical advancement with such a small engine had the result of increasing the performance of the machine to what seemed an incredible level for such a small engine.

Later, in September of the same year, a 90 cc step through model was introduced into the UK for the rider who needed a small reserve of power whilst retaining the same degree of rider protection.

As part of Honda's rationalisation programme the 70 cc step through model was introduced in February 1972, to replace both the 50 cc model and the 90 cc model, being an intermediate size to combine the most desirable features of both machines. Public demand for all three models was such, however, that the 50 cc and 90 cc models were not discontinued and are still currently available. Recently, introduction of 'moped legislation' has caused a decline in the sales of the 50 cc model but further legislation due shortly, may turn the tide of fortune.

General machine specifications

Model	C50	C70	C90
Overall length	1795 mm (70.67 in)	1795 mm (70.67 in)	1830 mm (72.10 in)
Overall width	640 mm (25.19 in)	640 mm (25.19 in)	640 mm (25.19 in)
Overall height	975 mm (38.4 in)	975 mm (38.4 in)	995 mm (39.2 in)
Wheelbase	1185 mm (46.65 in)	1185 mm (46.65 in)	1190 mm (46.89 in)
Ground clearance	130 mm (5.12 in)	130 mm (5.12 in)	130 mm (5.12 in)
Dry weight	68 kg (152 lb)	72 kg (159 lb)	85 kg (187 lb)

Ordering spare parts

When ordering spare parts for any of the Honda C50, C70 or C90 models, it is advisable to deal direct with an official Honda agent, who should be able to supply most items ex-stock. Parts cannot be obtained from Honda (UK) Limited direct; all orders must be routed via an approved agent, even if the parts required are not held in stock.

Always quote the engine and frame numbers in full, particularly if parts are required for any of the earlier models. The frame number is stamped on the left-hand side of the frame, close to the top mounting point of the engine unit. The engine number is stamped on the left-hand crankcase, immediately below the flywheel generator cover.

Use only parts of genuine Honda manufacture. Pattern parts are available, some of which originate from Japan and are packaged to resemble the originals. In many instances these parts will have an adverse effect on performance and/or reliability.

Some of the more expendable parts such as spark plugs, bulbs, tyres, oils and greases etc., can be obtained from accessory shops and motor factors, who have convenient opening hours, charge lower prices and can often be found not far from home. It is also possible to obtain parts on a Mail Order basis from a number of specialists who advertise regularly in the motor cycle magazines.

Frame number location

Engine number location

Safety first!

Professional motor mechanics are trained in safe working procedures. However enthusiastic you may be about getting on with the job in hand, do take the time to ensure that your safety is not put at risk. A moment's lack of attention can result in an accident, as can failure to observe certain elementary precautions.

There will always be new ways of having accidents, and the following points do not pretend to be a comprehensive list of all dangers; they are intended rather to make you aware of the risks and to encourage a safety-conscious approach to all work you carry out on your vehicle.

Essential DOs and DON'Ts

DON'T start the engine without first ascertaining that the transmission is in neutral.

DON'T suddenly remove the filler cap from a hot cooling system — cover it with a cloth and release the pressure gradually first, or you may get scalded by escaping coolant.

DON'T attempt to drain oil until you are sure it has cooled sufficiently to avoid scalding you.

DON'T grasp any part of the engine, exhaust or silencer without first ascertaining that it is sufficiently cool to avoid burning you.

DON'T allow brake fluid or antifreeze to contact the machine's paintwork or plastic components.

DON'T syphon toxic liquids such as fuel, brake fluid or antifreeze by mouth, or allow them to remain on your skin.

DON'T inhale dust — it may be injurious to health (see *Asbestos* heading).

DON'T allow any spilt oil or grease to remain on the floor — wipe it up straight away, before someone slips on it.

DON'T use ill-fitting spanners or other tools which may slip and cause injury.

DON'T attempt to lift a heavy component which may be beyond your capability — get assistance.

DON'T rush to finish a job, or take unverified short cuts.

DON'T allow children or animals in or around an unattended vehicle.

DON'T inflate a tyre to a pressure above the recommended maximum. Apart from overstressing the carcase and wheel rim, in extreme cases the tyre may blow off forcibly.

DO ensure that the machine is supported securely at all times. This is especially important when the machine is blocked up to aid wheel or fork removal.

DO take care when attempting to slacken a stubborn nut or bolt. It is generally better to pull on a spanner, rather than push, so that if slippage occurs you fall away from the machine rather than on to it.

DO wear eye protection when using power tools such as drill, sander, bench grinder etc.

DO use a barrier cream on your hands prior to undertaking dirty jobs — it will protect your skin from infection as well as making the dirt easier to remove afterwards; but make sure your hands aren't left slippery. Note that long-term contact with used engine oil can be a health hazard.

DO keep loose clothing (cuffs, tie etc) and long hair well out of the way of moving mechanical parts.

DO remove rings, wristwatch etc, before working on the vehicle — especially the electrical system.

DO keep your work area tidy — it is only too easy to fall over articles left lying around.

DO exercise caution when compressing springs for removal or installation. Ensure that the tension is applied and released in a controlled manner, using suitable tools which preclude the possibility of the spring escaping violently.

DO ensure that any lifting tackle used has a safe working load rating adequate for the job.

DO get someone to check periodically that all is well, when working alone on the vehicle.

DO carry out work in a logical sequence and check that everything is correctly assembled and tightened afterwards.

DO remember that your vehicle's safety affects that of yourself and others. If in doubt on any point, get specialist advice.

IF, in spite of following these precautions, you are unfortunate enough to injure yourself, seek medical attention as soon as possible.

Asbestos

Certain friction, insulating, sealing, and other products — such as brake linings, clutch linings, gaskets, etc — contain asbestos. *Extreme care must be taken to avoid inhalation of dust from such products since it is hazardous to health*. If in doubt, assume that they *do* contain asbestos.

Fire

Remember at all times that petrol (gasoline) is highly flammable. Never smoke, or have any kind of naked flame around, when working on the vehicle. But the risk does not end there — a spark caused by an electrical short-circuit, by two metal surfaces contacting each other, by careless use of tools, or even by static electricity built up in your body under certain conditions, can ignite petrol vapour, which in a confined space is highly explosive.

Always disconnect the battery earth (ground) terminal before working on any part of the fuel or electrical system, and never risk spilling fuel on to a hot engine or exhaust.

It is recommended that a fire extinguisher of a type suitable for fuel and electrical fires is kept handy in the garage or workplace at all times. Never try to extinguish a fuel or electrical fire with water.

Note: *Any reference to a 'torch' appearing in this manual should always be taken to mean a hand-held battery-operated electric lamp or flashlight. It does* **not** *mean a welding/gas torch or blowlamp.*

Fumes

Certain fumes are highly toxic and can quickly cause unconsciousness and even death if inhaled to any extent. Petrol (gasoline) vapour comes into this category, as do the vapours from certain solvents such as trichloroethylene. Any draining or pouring of such volatile fluids should be done in a well ventilated area.

When using cleaning fluids and solvents, read the instructions carefully. Never use materials from unmarked containers — they may give off poisonous vapours.

Never run the engine of a motor vehicle in an enclosed space such as a garage. Exhaust fumes contain carbon monoxide which is extremely poisonous; if you need to run the engine, always do so in the open air or at least have the rear of the vehicle outside the workplace.

The battery

Never cause a spark, or allow a naked light, near the vehicle's battery. It will normally be giving off a certain amount of hydrogen gas, which is highly explosive.

Always disconnect the battery earth (ground) terminal before working on the fuel or electrical systems.

If possible, loosen the filler plugs or cover when charging the battery from an external source. Do not charge at an excessive rate or the battery may burst.

Take care when topping up and when carrying the battery. The acid electrolyte, even when diluted, is very corrosive and should not be allowed to contact the eyes or skin.

If you ever need to prepare electrolyte yourself, always add the acid slowly to the water, and never the other way round. Protect against splashes by wearing rubber gloves and goggles.

Mains electricity and electrical equipment

When using an electric power tool, inspection light etc, always ensure that the appliance is correctly connected to its plug and that, where necessary, it is properly earthed (grounded). Do not use such appliances in damp conditions and, again, beware of creating a spark or applying excessive heat in the vicinity of fuel or fuel vapour. Also ensure that the appliances meet the relevant national safety standards.

Ignition HT voltage

A severe electric shock can result from touching certain parts of the ignition system, such as the HT leads, when the engine is running or being cranked, particularly if components are damp or the insulation is defective. Where an electronic ignition system is fitted, the HT voltage is much higher and could prove fatal.

Routine maintenance

Periodic routine maintenance is a continuous process that commences immediately the machine is used. It must be carried out at specified mileage recordings or on a calendar basis if the machine is not used frequently, whichever is sooner. Maintenance should be regarded as an insurance policy, to help keep the machine in the peak of condition and to ensure long, trouble-free service. It has the additional benefit of giving early warning of any faults that may develop and will act as a safety check, to the obvious advantage of both rider and machine alike.

The various maintenance tasks are described below, under their respective mileage and calendar headings. Accompanying diagrams are provided, where necessary. It should be remembered that the interval between the various maintenance tasks serves only as a guide. As the machine gets older or is used under particularly adverse conditions, it would be advisable to reduce the period between each check.

No special tools are required for the normal routine maintenance tasks. The tools contained in the toolkit supplied with every new machine are limited, but will suffice if the owner wishes to carry out only minor maintenance tasks.

When buying tools, it is worth spending a little more than the minimum to ensure that good quality tools are obtained. Some of the cheaper tools are too soft or flimsy to do an adequate job. It is infuriating to have to stop part way through a job because a spanner has splayed open or broken, and a replacement must be found.

A deep rooted knowledge of engineering principle is by no means necessary before the owner undertakes his or her own maintenance tasks but familiarity with a few of the more commonly used terms and a basic knowledge of how to use tools will help.

The following list of tools will suffice to undertake the routine maintenance tasks described in this Section, but where reference is made to another Chapter for the dismantling procedure, additional tools may be required.

> *A tyre pressure gauge.*
> *A tyre pump*
> *A 10 mm or 12 mm spark plug spanner*
> *A set of metric open ended spanners from 6 mm to 17 mm*
> *A pair of pliers*
> *Two cross head screwdrivers, size 2 and 3*
> *A small electrical screwdriver*
> *A set of feeler gauges*
> *A 23 mm box or ring spanner*
> *A 3 mm square socket (Honda tool)*
> *An adjustable spanner (this tool to be used only as a last resort)*

Weekly or every 200 miles (320 km)

1 Check the tyre pressures
The tyre pressure should be 26 psi for the front tyre and 29 psi for the rear tyre measured when the tyres are cold.

Remove the dust cap, flick the valve centre to blow out any dirt or water and push on the pressure gauge. If the pressure is too low, pump up the tyre with the pump or a garage air line to the correct pressure. If the pressure is too high, push the valve centre to release the air until the correct pressure is reached. Replace the dust cap as it is a second seal.

Check the tyre pressures

2 Check the engine oil level
The engine oil capacity is 0.8 litres C50 model, 0.7 litre C70 model and 0.9 litre C90 model (1.4, 1.2 and 1.6 pints respectively) contained in a wet sump, and normally SAE 20W/50 but in a cold climate SAE 10W/30 should be used.

Crankcase dipstick

DIPSTICK

Maximum oil level

Minimum oil level

Place the machine on its centre stand on level ground. If the machine has just been run, allow the oil to settle for 5 minutes before checking the level. Remove the plastic filler cap with its integral dipstick. Wipe the oil off the dipstick. Replace the dipstick without screwing it in, remove it and check that the oil level is between the upper and lower limit marks on the dipstick. Add oil if necesssary, to bring the oil to the correct level, and replace the filler cap dipstick after ensuring that the sealing O-ring is in good condition.

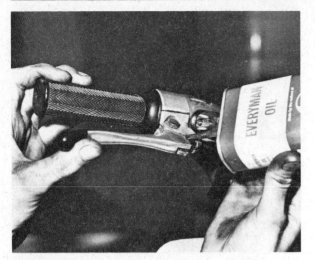

Oiling the front brake lever

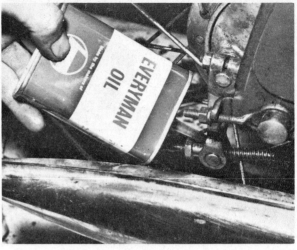

Oiling the rear brake adjuster

- Nipple
- Inner cable
- Plasticine funnel around outer cable
- Cable suspended vertically
- Cable is lubricated when oil drops from far end

Oiling a control cable

Frame is marked to aid wheel alignment

3 Oil and adjust the brake cables and rod

The standard brake cables should be lubricated with a light machine oil, but if a nylon lined cable has been fitted on no account use oil on it.

Similarly, the cable nipples and pivot points should be oiled including those of the brake rod. Normally, rain and the washing of the machine will provide sufficient lubrication for the nylon and plastic parts. Before the winter sets in each year, it is advisable to remove the cables completely and thoroughly lubricate them as shown in the accompanying sketch, to ensure troublefree riding during the more arduous conditions to be found in winter..

The brakes need adjusting when there is too much movement on the lever or the pedal ie; when the brake lever comes close to the handlebar when the brake is applied or if there is too much movement of the brake pedal. To adjust either brake turn the adjusting nut until the brake just starts to rub when the wheel is spun. Slacken back the adjusting nut until the brake just stops rubbing. Ensure that the adjusting nut cut-outs are seating correctly on the brake operating arms.

4 Check, adjust and lubricate the final drive chain

Place the machine on its centre stand on level ground. Check the up and down movement of the chain, midway between the two sprockets. Rotate the back wheel until the up and down movement is at the minimum. This is the 'tight spot' on the chain and the up and down movement here should be between 10 mm (0.40 inch) and 20 mm (0.79 inch).

If the play is greater than 20 mm (0.79 inch) the chain should be adjusted as follows:

Slacken the wheel spindle nuts so that they are finger tight. Make sure that each adjusting nut is turned the same amount, to keep the wheels in line, until the play is reduced to within the limits. Tighten the wheel spindle nuts and recheck the amount of play on the chain.

When the wheels are properly aligned both the adjusters should match the swinging arm markings.

An SAE 90 oil or a Chain Lubricant should be spread on the chain for lubrication. The latter is applied from an aerosol pack, to make application easier.

5 Check the lights and horn

Check that all the lights are working properly. Renew any defective bulbs and if any lights are dim, clean the connections and earthing points, to restore the lights to their original brightness.

Check that the horn works, again checking the connections if the performance is poor.

6 Visual inspection

Give the whole machine a close visual inspection, checking for loose nuts and fittings, frayed control cables or missing parts which may have fallen off or been stolen.

Lubricating the chain

The larger bolt is the drain plug

7 Check the battery

Remove the side panel, release the battery and slide it out. Remove the top cover, if fitted, and unscrew the three vent plugs on top of the plates. On translucent batteries, the level of the liquid is marked on the outside of the battery. If the liquid level is low, the three separate cells in the battery should be topped up to the correct level with distilled water. Tap water should not be used as the impurities in the water will have an adverse effect on the battery life.

Replace the three plugs and the cover and refit the battery to the machine, finally replacing the side panel.

If any liquid is spilt out of the battery this should be washed off immediately with plenty of water as it will corrode any metal parts and burn the skin if left unattended.

Monthly or every 1000 miles (1600 km)

Check the tyres, brakes, lights and horn as described in the weekly/200 miles service and then carry out the following additional tasks:

1 Change the engine oil

As stated previously the engine oil capacity is between 0.7 and 0.9 litres (1.3 and 1.6 pints) of SAE 20W/50 oil, the precise quantity depending on the model.

Place the machine on its centre stand on level ground. Run the engine for a few minutes to warm up the oil so that it will run out easier. Place a container under the engine and remove the drain plug, which is situated on the underside of the engine. When all the oil has drained, replace and tighten the drain plug, ensuring that the sealing washer is in good condition.

Refill the engine with oil of the correct viscosity, checking the level as described in the weekly check.

2 Check the spark plug

An NGK type C-7HS or D-6HN spark plug is fitted as standard equipment to the Honda C50, C70 and C90. The recommended gap of the plug is 0.6 mm (0.024 inch) to 0.7 mm (0.028 inch).

Pull off the spark plug cap and unscrew the plug. Clean the electrode to remove any oil or carbon. Check the gap between the electrode with a set of feeler gauges. If the gap needs resetting, bend the outer electrode to bring it closer to the central electrode. Do not try to move the centre electrode as the insulation will break and ruin the plug.

Refit the spark plug and push on the plug cap. Do not over-tighten the spark plug as this can cause the thread to strip in the cylinder head. A normal plug spanner has the correct length tommy bar or handle to make overtightening impossible.

A new spark plug should be fitted every 5,000 miles (8,000 km), or if it is damaged or excessively worn.

3 Check and adjust the throttle cable

The throttle should have about 10° free play movement. To adjust the amount of free play, slide the rubber sleeve cable, to reveal the adjusting nut. The adjusting nut is turned to provide the correct play and the rubber sleeve, when slid back down the cable, stops the adjusting nut from turning.

4 Check and adjust the carburettor slow running adjustment

Any checks or adjustments that are made on the carburettor should be undertaken only when the engine has reached its normal working temperature and not when the engine is cold.

The engine should continue to run slowly when the throttle is closed. If the engine stops every time the throttle is closed, adjustment is necessary. As the machine has an automatic clutch, if the engine runs too fast, the machine will tend to creep forward when it is in gear unless the brakes are applied to stop it.

Slacken the throttle cable to ensure that there is plenty of slack so that cable tension does not give false adjustment on the carburettor.

On the side of the carburettor are two screws, the upper one is the throttle stop screw, the lower the air mixture screw.

To adjust the slow running of the engine, turn the throttle stop screw until the engine is running at approximately 1500 rpm.

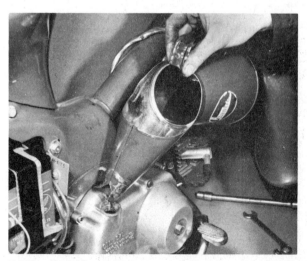

Refilling the engine with oil

Turn the air mixture screw until the highest engine speed is obtained. If the engine speed is then too fast, unscrew the throttle stop screw to reduce it, then turn the air mixture screw to find the highest engine speed again. This process is repeated until the engine runs slowly and evenly. Readjust the throttle cable slack to the limit as set out under the previous heading.

5   *Check the tyre condition*

By law a motorcycle must have a minimum depth of tread of 1 mm (0.04 inch) for at least 75% of the tyre width all the way round the circumference of the tyre. In the interest of safety it is better to renew the tyre long before the legal minimum is reached.

When checking the tyre condition, remove any stones in the tread, check for any bulges, splits or bald spots and renew the tyre if any doubt exists by following the procedure given in Chapter 6 , Section 17.

6   *Check the clutch adjustment*

The clutch plates will wear inside the clutch and the adjustment should be checked periodically to ensure that smooth gearchanging continues.

Clutch adjustment is provided by means of an adjustable screw and locknut located in the centre of the clutch cover. Slacken off the 10 mm locknut and turn the adjusting screw firstly in a clockwise direction, to ensure there is no end pressure on the clutch pushrod.

Turn the adjusting screw anticlockwise until pressure can be felt on the end. Turn back (clockwise) for approximately 1/8th of a turn, and tighten the locknut, making sure the screw does not turn. Clutch adjustment should now be correct.

Six monthly or every 3,000 miles (5,000 km)

Complete all the checks under the weekly and monthly headings and then the following items.

1   *Clean the air filter*

The air filter is located on top of the main frame tube, immediately behind the steering head, clearly visible when the legshield has been removed.

To clean the air filter, remove the detachable element and tap it lightly to remove accumulated dust. Blow dry from the inside with compressed air, or brush the exterior with a light brush. Remember the element is made from paper. If it is torn or damaged, fit a replacement.

Oil or water will reduce the efficiency of the filter element and may upset the carburettor. Replace any suspect element.

It is advisable to replace the element at less than the recommended 6,000 miles if the machine is used in very dusty conditions. The usual signs of a filter element in need of eplacement are reduced performance, misfiring and a tendency for the carburation to run rich.

On no account should the machine be run without the filter element in place because this will have an adverse effect on carburation. Reassembly of the air filter is the reverse of the dismantling procedure.

2   *Clean the carburettor and filter*

Over a period of time sediment and water will collect in the carburettor. A drain screw on the carburettor enables the float chamber to be flushed out with petrol to remove nearly all of the dirt but Chapter 3 Sections 7 to 10 will describe how the carburettor itself is removed, stripped, cleaned and reassembled, if any trouble still persists.

3   *Remove, clean and lubricate the final drive chain*

Although the final drive chain is fully enclosed, the oil and grease lubricant on the chain will tend to pick up dust and grit, so every six months it is advisable to remove the chain from the machine for thorough cleaning.

To remove the chain, place the machine on its centre stand on level ground, remove the four bolts and the two chaincase halves and rotate the rear wheel until the spring link is in a convenient position, preferably on the rear wheel sprocket. Use a pair of pliers to remove the spring clip and then remove the side plate and the link plate, thus disconnecting the chain.

Connect to one end of the chain a second chain, either an old worn out one or a brand new one which is kept in readiness for fitting to the machine. Pull the first chain off the machine, feeding the second chain on, until the first chain can be disconnected from the second chain. If the second chain is usable, reconnect it, ensuring that the closed end of the spring clip is facing the direction of travel of the chain. Adjust the chain as described in the weekly maintenance section and refit the chaincase.

The chain which has just been removed should be washed thoroughly in petrol or paraffin to remove all the dirt and grease.

To check whether the chain is due for renewal, lay it lengthwise in a straight line and compress it so that all play is taken up. Anchor one end and then pull on the other end to take up the play in the opposite direction. If the chain extends by more than the distance between two adjacent links, it should be renewed in conjunction with the sprockets.

The chain should be lubricated by immersing it in a molten lubricant such as Linklyfe or Chainguard and then hanging it up to drain. This will ensure good penetration of lubricant between the pins and rollers, which is less likely to be thrown off when the chain is in motion.

To refit the chain to the machine, connect it to the second chain, pull the second chain and feed the first chain back onto the machine. Reconnect the chain ensuring the spring clip is correctly fitted as stated before. It is easier to reconnect the chain if the ends are fitted onto the rear wheel sprocket whilst the connecting link is inserted. Adjust the chain, using the weekly maintenance procedure, and refit the chaincase.

4   *Check and adjust the valve tappet clearances*

The valve tappet clearance for both the inlet and exhaust valves is 0.05 mm (0.002 inch) when the engine is cold.

A small amount of dismantling is required before the tappet clearance can be checked.

Ensure that the machine is on its centre stand, standing on level ground. Remove the flywheel inspection cover on the left-hand side of the engine. Remove also the two tappet covers to reveal the adjusters.

To check the tappet clearances, turn the flywheel until the line marked with a'T' is aligned with the mark on the flywheel cover. The piston will now be at top dead centre on either the compression or exhaust stroke. Checking the tappet clearances must be made on the compression stroke when both rocker arms are free to rock, so a complete turn of the flywheel is required if the piston is on the exhaust stroke. It will probably be found that when turning the flywheel, the 'T' mark tends to move on every other revolution when the piston is under compression. This is the position required for checking the tappet clearances and to avoid the 'T' mark moving, removing the spark plug and its cover will relieve the pressure in the cylinder.

A 0.05 mm (0.002 inch) feeler gauge should just pass between the rocker arm and the valve stem. If adjustment is necessary, slacken the locking nut and turn the adjusting screw until the feeler gauge will just pass through the gap. Hold the adjusting screw securely and retighten the locknut. Check the gap again to ensure that it is still correct. This applies to both valves as the clearance is identical.

Refit the tappet covers, checking the condition of the O-rings. Refit the spark plug, the plug cover and the flywheel cover, unless the next task of checking the ignition timing is about to be carried out.

5   *Check and adjust the ignition timing*

C50 and C70 models only: The ignition timing is determined by when the contact breaker points open. The flywheel operates the contact breaker and the heel of the contact arm will wear, altering the ignition timing. The flywheel inspection cover should be removed so that the contact breaker can be viewed through one of the apertures in the flywheel. When the line marked 'F' on the flywheel lines up with the mark on the crankcase shaft, the contact breaker should just start to open. If adjustment is necessary, the fixed contact can be moved by slackening the clamping screw and using a screwdriver in the slot provided. Retighten the clamping screw and check the adjustment again, to ensure that it has not altered.

Align the 'T' mark with the mark on the cover

Use a feeler gauge to check the gap

Align the 'F' mark with the mark on the cover

When the ignition timing is correct, rotate the flywheel to determine the position at which the contact breaker points are fully open. When fully open the contact breaker gap should be between 0.3 mm and 0.4 mm (0.012 and 0.016 in).

If the gap is too small, the contact breaker points need renewing, as described in Chapter 4 Section 6.

Refit the flywheel cover and the spark plug and plug cover, if these have been removed.

C90 model only: The ignition timing is determined by when the contact breaker points open. The camshaft operates the contact breaker and the heel of the contact arm will wear, altering the ignition timing. The flywheel inspection cover and the contact breaker cover must be removed. Before checking the ignition timing, the contact breaker gap should be checked. Rotate the engine until the contact breaker is in its fully open position. Check the gap to see if it is between 0.3 and 0.4 mm (0.012 and 0.016 inch). To adjust the gap, slacken the two screws that hold the contact breaker assembly, and using a small screwdriver in the slot provided ease the assembly to the correct position. Tighten the screws and recheck the gap to ensure that the assembly has not moved.

The ignition timing is correct when the contact breaker points are about to separate when the 'F' line scribed on the flywheel rotor coincides exactly with the mark on the cover. The backplate holding the complete contact breaker assembly is slotted, to permit a limited range of adjustment. If the two crosshead retaining screws are slackened a little, the plate can be turned until the points commence to separate, and then locked in this position by tightening the screws.

After checking the timing, rotate the engine and check again before replacing the covers. The accuracy of the ignition timing is critical in terms of both engine performance and petrol consumption. Even a small error in setting can have a noticeable effect on both.

6 *Check the centre and prop stand springs*

Check the condition of the centre and prop stand springs and renew them if they are worn or heavily corroded. If the stand drops when the machine is moving, it may catch in some obstacle in the road and unseat the rider. Grease the springs and the stand pivot points.

7 *Grease the speedometer cable*

Once the headlamp lens has been removed the speedometer cable can be unscrewed from the speedometer head and pulled clear. The inner cable can then be pulled out. Clean off the old grease by washing in petrol or paraffin. Spread new grease along the length of the cable except for the top 15 cm (6 inch) and feed the cable back into the outer casing. Reconnect the cable to the speedometer head.

Check the return spring condition

Greasing the suspension pivots

Greasing the leading link fork pivots

Remove the switch assembly to release the twistgrip

Slide the twistgrip off for greasing

Remove the sliding block to oil the cable

Oil the felt wick

If the top of the cable is greased, the grease will work its way into the speedometer head and stop it functioning, thus necessitating a replacement as the speedometer head cannot be stripped for cleaning.

8 Grease the leading link forks

Apply a grease gun to the nipples on the leading links and the fork blades. Pump grease into the bearings until clean grease emerges from the joints. Wipe away any excess grease as this will collect the dirt and make the machine look unsightly.

9 Grease the throttle twistgrip and oil the throttle cable

Remove the two screws and the indicator switch from the handlebar. This releases the twisting sleeve which slides off the handlebar with an anti-clockwise twist. The sliding block can now be lifted out of the handlebar and the inner cable unhooked. The outer cable stop can then be removed from the handlebar and unhooked from the cable.

10 Adjust the camshaft chain tension

Before attempting to adjust the camshaft chain tension, it should be noted that three different types of camshaft chain tensioner assembly are used within the range of models, one being of an automatic type and the other two being of a manual type. To recognise the automatic tensioner, look for a blank sealing plug with a hexagon-shaped head located on the forward part of the underside of the left-hand crankcase. A similar sealing plug exists for one of the manual tensioners but this is accompanied by a slotted adjuster stud and locknut located just forward of the gearchange pedal shaft. The remaining type of manual tensioner may be recognised by the slotted end of the adjuster screw which is visible in the centre of a sealing plug which takes the place of the blank types previously described. Reference should be made to Figs. 1.13 and 1.14 of Chapter 1 when determining the type of tensioner fitted. Details of removing and inspecting the component parts of the automatic tensioner are given in Section 33 of Chapter 1; the method of adjusting the manual tensioners being as follows.

Before adjustment of either type of manual tensioner is made, the engine should be started and allowed to run until it reaches normal operating temperature. With the engine set to idle at 1500 ± 100 rpm, proceed to adjust the type of tensioner fitted as follows.

Where the tensioner is of the type with the slotted adjuster screw located in the centre of the sealing plug, adjustment is made simply by unscrewing the screw approximately ¼ of a turn. This allows the two collars within the tensioner to release their grip on the guide rod, thus allowing the rod to move under pressure from the spring; this in turn pushes the pushrod against the tensioner ring thereby tensioning the chain. Retighten the adjuster screw and the adjustment is complete.

The remaining type of manual tensioner is adjusted by loosening the locknut located just forward of the gearchange pedal shaft and unscrewing the screw approximately 1½ turns.

This will release the pushrod and allow it to bear against the tensioner arm under pressure from the springs, thereby tensioning the chain. Complete the adjustment procedure by tightening both the screw and locknut. If excessive noise from the chain persists, then the screw and locknut should be left loose and the sealing plug removed from the crankcase to allow access to the slotted adjuster located beneath it. Screw in this adjuster until the noise from the chain ceases and then retighten the screw and locknut. Before refitting the sealing plug, screw in on the slotted adjuster to preload the tensioner spring. This will make any subsequent adjustment easier in that it will only be necessary to loosen and retighten the locknut and screw. It should be noted that additional pre-load will not diminish the noise produced by a badly worn chain and cam sprockets. The additional adjustment facility provided should be used only for removal of noise caused by a slack chain in good condition.

Yearly or every 5,000 miles (8,000 km)

Complete all the checks listed under the weekly, monthly and six monthly headings, then complete the following additional tasks:

1 Lubricate the felt wick of the contact breaker cam

When the ignition timing is checked, the felt wick of the contact breaker cam can be seen. A few drops of light machine oil, should be put on the wick to reduce wear on the heel of the contact arm. Do not over oil. If oil finds its way on to the contact breaker points it will act as an insulator and prevent electrical contact from being made.

2 Check the condition of the sprockets

When the final drive chain is cleaned and checked, ensure that the sprockets are not badly worn, before replacing the chain. If the sprocket teeth are badly worn, they will probably have a hooked appearance and should be renewed as described in Chapter 1 Sections 16 and 47 and Chapter 6 Section 12.

3 Adjust and lubricate the steering head bearings

Dismantling and reassembly of the steering head is a task that should be undertaken only if a good understanding of the problems involved is realised. Chapter 5 Sections 2 and 4, fully describe the necessary procedures.

4 Examine and lubricate the wheel bearings

Dismantling and reassembly of the wheel bearings is also a task to be undertaking only if an understanding of the problems involved is realised. Chapter 6 fully describes the necessary procedure.

5 Examine both front and rear brake assemblies

The brake assemblies should be cleaned to remove any dust and checked to ensure that the brake linings are not wearing too thin. This task is fully described in Chapter 6.

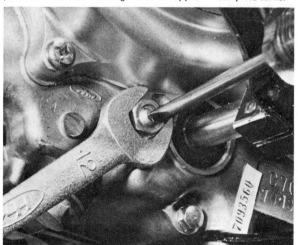

Release the tensioner pushrod by unscrewing the locknut and screw

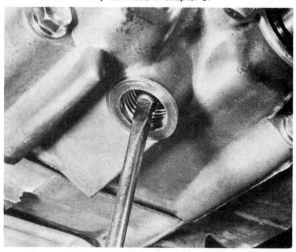

Screw in on the adjuster until chain noise ceases

Recommended lubricants

Engine
Normal temperature   ...   .   Multi-grade 20W/50 engine oil
Below freezing point   ...   .   Multi-grade 10W/30 engine oil

Final drive chain   ...   .   Graphited grease or aerosol type chain lubricant

All greasing points   ...   .   Multi-purpose high melting point lithium-based grease

Oil points   ...   .   Light oil

The engine oil should be changed every 1,000 miles. In winter, or when the machine is used for short journeys only, the oil must be changed every 300 miles.

Working conditions and tools

When a major overhaul is contemplated, it is important that a clean, well-lit working space is available, equipped with a workbench and vice, and with space for laying out or storing the dismantled assemblies in an orderly manner where they are unlikely to be disturbed. The use of a good workshop will give the satisfaction of work done in comfort and without haste, where there is little chance of the machine being dismantled and reassembled in anything other than clean surroundings. Unfortunately, these ideal working conditions are not always practicable and under these latter circumstances when improvisation is called for, extra care and time will be needed.

The other essential requirement is a comprehensive set of good quality tools. Quality is of prime importance since cheap tools will prove expensive in the long run if they slip or break when in use, causing personal injury or expensive damage to the component being worked on. A good quality tool will last a long time, and more than justify the cost.

For practically all tools, a tool factor is the best source since he will have a very comprehensive range compared with the average garage or accessory shop. Having said that, accessory shops often offer excellent quality tools at discount prices, so it pays to shop around. There are plenty of tools around at reasonable prices, but always aim to purchase items which meet the relevant national safety standards. If in doubt, seek the advice of the shop proprietor or manager before making a purchase.

The basis of any tool kit is a set of open-ended spanners, which can be used on almost any part of the machine to which there is reasonable access. A set of ring spanners makes a useful addition, since they can be used on nuts that are very tight or where access is restricted. Where the cost has to be kept within reasonable bounds, a compromise can be effected with a set of combination spanners – open-ended at one end and having a ring of the same size on the other end. Socket spanners may also be considered a good investment; a basic 3/8 in or 1/2 in drive kit comprising a ratchet handle and a small number of socket heads, if money is limited. Additional sockets can be purchased, as and when they are required. Provided they are slim in profile, sockets will reach nuts or bolts that are deeply recessed. When purchasing spanners of any kind, make sure the correct size standard is purchased. Almost all machines manufactured outside the UK and the USA have metric nuts and bolts, whilst those produced in Britain have BSF or BSW sizes. The standard used in USA is AF, which is also found on some of the later British machines. Others tools that should be included in the kit are a range of crosshead screwdrivers, a pair of pliers and a hammer.

When considering the purchase of tools, it should be remembered that by carrying out the work oneself, a large proportion of the normal repair cost, made up by labour charges, will be saved. The economy made on even a minor overhaul will go a long way towards the improvement of a toolkit.

In addition to the basic tool kit, certain additional tools can prove invaluable when they are close to hand, to help speed up a multitude of repetitive jobs. For example, an impact screwdriver will ease the removal of screws that have been tightened by a similar tool, during assembly, without a risk of damaging the screw heads. And, of course, it can be used again to retighten the screws, to ensure an oil or airtight seal results. Circlip pliers have their uses too, since gear pinions, shafts and similar components are frequently retained by circlips that are not too easily displaced by a screwdriver. There are two types of circlip pliers, one for internal and one for external circlips. They may also have straight or right-angled jaws.

One of the most useful of all tools is the torque wrench, a form of spanner that can be adjusted to slip when a measured amount of force is applied to any bolt or nut. Torque wrench settings are given in almost every modern workshop or service manual, where the extent to which a complex component, such as a cylinder head, can be tightened without fear of distortion or leakage. The tightening of bearing caps is yet another example. Overtightening will stretch or even break bolts, necessitating extra work to extract the broken portions.

As may be expected, the more sophisticated the machine, the greater is the number of tools likely to be required if it is to be kept in first class condition by the home mechanic. Unfortunately there are certain jobs which cannot be accomplished successfully without the correct equipment and although there is invariably a specialist who will undertake the work for a fee, the home mechanic will have to dig more deeply in his pocket for the purchase of similar equipment if he does not wish to employ the services of others. Here a word of caution is necessary, since some of these jobs are best left to the expert. Although an electrical multimeter of the AVO type will prove helpful in tracing electrical faults, in inexperienced hands it may irrevocably damage some of the electrical components if a test current is passed through them in the wrong direction. This can apply to the synchronisation of twin or multiple carburettors too, where a certain amount of expertise is needed when setting them up with vacuum gauges. These are, however, exceptions. Some instruments, such as a strobe lamp, are virtually essential when checking the timing of a machine powered by CDI ignition system. In short, do not purchase any of these special items unless you have the experience to use them correctly.

Although this manual shows how components can be removed and replaced without the use of special service tools (unless absolutely essential), it is worthwhile giving consideration to the purchase of the more commonly used tools if the machine is regarded as a long term purchase Whilst the alternative methods suggested will remove and replace parts without risk of damage, the use of the special tools recommended and sold by the manufacturer will invariably save time.

Chapter 1 Engine and gearbox

Contents

Specifications

Engine

Type	Single cylinder overhead camshaft, chain operated
Cylinder head	Aluminium alloy
Cylinder barrel	Cast iron
Bore	39 mm (C50)
	47 mm (C70)
	50 mm (C90)
Stroke	41.4 mm (C50 and C70)
	45.6 mm (C90)
Capacity	49 cc (C50)
	72 cc (C70)
	89.6 cc (C90)
Bhp	4.8 @ 10,000 rpm (C50)
	6.2 @ 9,000 rpm (C70)
	7.5 @ 9,500 rpm (C90)

Compression ratio ... ...   8.1 : 1 (C70)
8.2 : 1 (C90)
8.8 : 1 (C50)

Crankshaft
Crankpin outside diameter ... ...   23.098 - 23.112 mm (0.9099 - 0.9105 inch)

Connecting rod
Big-end end float ... ...   0.1 - 0.35 mm (0.004 - 0.014 inch)
Small end and gudgeon pin clearance ... ...   0.025 - 0.050 mm (0.001 - 0.002 inch)
Small end bore diameter ... ...   13.016 - 13.043 mm (0.5124 - 0.5135 inch)
(50 and 70 cc models)
14.012 - 14.028 mm (0.5517 - 0.5523 inch)
(90 cc model)

Piston
Maximum diameter at base of skirt ... ...   38.98 - 39.00 mm (1.5392 - 1.5400 inch)
(50 cc model)
46.98 - 47.00 mm (1.8492 - 1.8500 inch)
(70 cc model)
49.97 - 49.99 mm (1.9673 - 1.9681 inch)
(90 cc model)
Piston to cylinder clearance (minimum) ... ...   0.01 mm (0.0004 inch)
Replace if over 0.1 mm (0.004 inch)
Oversize pistons available ... ...   +0.25 mm, +0.50 mm, +0.75 mm and +1.00 mm
Piston gudgeon pin clearance ... ...   0.002 - 0.014 mm (0.00008 - 0.00055 inch)

Piston rings
Compression (two top rings) ... ...   Top ring chrome, second ring tapered
Oil control ring ... ...   Third ring at top of skirt

Gudgeon pin
Diameter ... ...   13.002 - 13.008 mm (0.5121 - 0.5123 inch)

Valves
Tappet clearance, inlet and exhaust ... ...   0.05 mm (0.002 inch) set with engine cold
Seat angle ... ...   45°
Inlet, overall length ... ...   64.5 mm (2.540 inch) (70 cc model)
66 mm (2.600 inch) (50 cc model)
67.3 mm (2.648 inch) (90 cc model)
Outside diameter of stem ... ...   5.5 mm (0.217 inch) (50 and 70 cc models)
5.45 mm (0.215 inch) (90 cc model)
Exhaust, overall length ... ...   63.9 mm (2.483 inch) (70 cc model)
65.3 mm (2.573 inch) (50 cc model)
67.3 mm (2.597 inch) (90 cc model)
Ouside diameter of stem ... ...   5.5 mm (0.217 inch) (50 and 70 cc models)
5.43 mm (0.214 inch) (90 cc model)
Stem and guide clearance (inlet) ... ...   0.010 - 0.030 mm (0.0004 - 0.0012 inch)
Stem and guide clearance (exhaust) ... ...   0.030 - 0.050 mm (0.0012 - 0.0020 inch)
Spring (outer) free length ... ...   28.1 mm (1.110 inch) (50 and 70 cc models)
31.8 mm (1.253 inch) (90 cc model)
Spring (inner) free length ... ...   25.5 mm (1.01 inch) (50 and 70 cc models)
26.5 mm (1.044 inch) (90 cc model)

Capacities
Engine and gearbox (in unit) ... ...   50 cc model   0.8 litres (1.4 Imp pints) (1.7 US pints)
70 cc model   0.7 litres (1.2 Imp pints) (1.5 US pints)
90 cc model   0.9 litres (1.58 Imp pints) (1.90 US pints)

Torque wrench settings
Cylinder head nuts ... ...   6.5 - 8.7 ft lb
Cylinder head left side cover ... ...   5.8 - 8.7 ft lb
Cylinder head right-hand side cover ... ...   5.1 - 6.5 lb ft
Carburettor mounting studs ... ...   60 in lb
Flywheel nut ... ...   23.9 - 27.5 ft lb
Clutch nut ... ...   27.5 - 32.5 lb ft

1 General description

The Honda C50, C70 and C90 models are fitted with an overhead camshaft engine in which the valve mechanism is chain driven. The camshaft is located within the aluminium alloy cylinder head; with this arrangement it is necessary to disturb the valve timing when the cylinder head is removed.

All engine/gear units are of aluminium alloy construction, with a cast iron cylinder barrel. The flywheel generator is mounted on the left-hand side of the engine unit; the clutch assembly is located on the right-hand side of the engine, behind a domed aluminium alloy cover. Convention is defied by installing the engine /gear unit in a near-horizontal position, so that the cylinder barrel is almost parallel to the ground. The exhaust system is carried on the right-hand side of the machine, of the down-swept pattern. All models are fitted with a conventional kickstart.

A trochoid oil pump is included in the general specification of the engine, to provide a pressure oil feed in addition to lubrication by splash. There are also two filters in the lubrication system, a gauze screen in the crankcase and a centrifugal filter within the clutch centre.

The engine is built in unit with the gearbox. This means that when the engine is dismantled, the gearbox has to be dismantled too, and vice-versa.

2 Operations with engine/gearbox in frame

It is not necessary to remove the engine unit from the frame unless the crankshaft assembly and/or the gearbox bearings require attention. Most operations can be accomplished with the engine in place, such as:
1 Removal and replacement of cylinder head.
2 Removal and replacement of cylinder barrel and piston.
3 Removal and replacement of flywheel magnetic generator.
4 Removal and replacement of clutch assembly.
5 Removal and replacement of timing pinions and kickstart assembly.

When several operations need to be undertaken simultaneously, it will probably be advantageous to remove the complete engine unit from the frame, an operation that should take approximately twenty minutes. This will give the advantage of better access and more working space.

3 Operations with engine/gearbox removed

1 Removal and replacement of the main bearings.
2 Removal and replacement of the crankshaft assembly.
3 Removal and replacement of the gear cluster, selectors and gearbox main bearings.

4 Method of engine/gearbox removal

As described previously, the engine and gearbox are built in unit and it is necessary to remove the complete unit in order to gain access to either component. Separation is accomplished after the engine unit has been removed and refitting cannot take place until the crankcase has been reassembled.

5 Removing the engine/gearbox unit

1 Place the machine on the centre stand and make sure it is standing firmly, on level ground.
2 Remove the side panels to obtain the tool kit and reveal the battery. Unscrew the fuse holder and remove the fuse, to isolate the battery.
3 Remove the domed nut and the air cleaner lid and withdraw the element.

5.3 Remove the air cleaner lid

5.4a Slacken the nuts and remove the clamping band ...

5.4b ... followed by the other bolts and spacers

5.6 Release the exhaust pipe from the cylinder

5.8 Remove the gearchange lever

5.10 Disconnect the wires at the snap connectors

5.11 Remove the spark plug cap and HT lead clip

5.12 Disconnect the brake and stoplight springs

4   Slacken the nuts holding the rear of the plastic legshields and remove the clamping band, if fitted. Remove the four bolts holding the legshields and pull their spacers clear. The legshields will now lift clear, allowing easy access to the engine.

5   Remove the crankcase drain plug and drain the oil into a suitable container.

6   Remove the two nuts holding the exhaust pipe to the cylinder head and unscrew the swinging arm pivot nut to release the silencer. The exhaust system will then pull clear, pulling the two collets out of the cylinder head. Remove the copper/asbestos joint ring from the exhaust port.

7   Ensure that the petrol is switched off and remove the nuts clamping the carburettor to the cylinder head. The carburettor can be left in place when the engine is dropped out of the frame.

8   Remove the gearchange lever clamp bolt and slide the lever off its shaft.

9   Remove the three screws and the flywheel generator cover or two screws and rear cover on the C90 model, to reveal the final drive sprocket. Rotate the rear wheel until the chain spring link is in a removable position. Disconnect the chain at the spring link and pull the chain clear of the engine sprocket. If the chain is reconnected, it will ease finding both ends of the chain when reassembling. It may be necessary to remove two bolts and the top half of the chainguard to obtain greater access to the chain.

10 Pull the snap connectors apart to disconnect the engine wires. All of them are colour coded for easy reconnection.

11 Pull off the spark plug cap and remove the screw to release the HT lead.

12 Unhook the brake pedal and stop lamp switch springs.

13 Remove the footrest assembly, which is attached to the crankcase by four 14 mm bolts and spring washers. It is possible to remove the engine/gear unit with the footrests in place, if it is desired to use them as a convenient carrying handle.

14 Remove the top engine bolt and allow the engine to pivot down. Ensure that the carburettor has slid off its studs and is clear of the engine. Remove the bottom engine bolt and pull the engine clear of the machine. Note that the C90 model has an inlet tube bolted to the cylinder head which can either be removed or left attached to the carburettor.

5.14a Remove the top engine bolt ...

6 Dismantling the engine and gearbox: general

Before commencing work on the engine unit, the external surface should be cleaned thoroughly. A motor cycle engine has very little protection from road grit and other foreign matter, which will find its way into the dismantled engine if this simple precaution is not observed. One of the proprietary engine cleaning compounds such as 'Gunk' or 'Jizer' can be used to good effect particularly if the compound is allowed to work into the film of grease and oil before it is washed away. When washing down, make sure that water cannot enter the carburettor or the electrical system, particularly if these parts have been exposed.

Never use undue force to remove any stubborn part, unless mention is made of this requirement. There is invariable good reason why a part is difficult to remove, often because the dismantling operation has been tackled in the wrong sequence.

Dismantling will be made easier if a simple engine stand is constructed that will correspond with the engine mounting points. This arrangement will permit the complete unit to be clamped rigidly to the work bench, leaving both hands free.

7 Dismantling the engine and gearbox: removal of generator

Engine in the frame

As stated in Section 2 of this Chapter, it is possible to remove the generator whilst the engine is still in the frame. Only paragraphs 1 to 5, 8 and 10 of Section 5 need to be completed before proceeding with the following dismantling procedure:

5.14b ... followed by the bottom engine bolt

7.2 Remove the rotor nut

7.3 Method for removing the rotor when special service tool is not available

7.4 Release the wire on the neutral switch

7.6 Remove the stator plate and take care not to lose the Woodruff key

8.2 Remove the circular cover

Engine removed from the frame

If the whole of Section 5 has been completed, continue with the following dismantling procedure:

C50 and C70 models only

1   Remove the three screws and the generator cover.
2   Hold the generator securely and remove the central nut and washer.
3   Use a Honda extractor tool to remove the rotor as it is a keyed taper fit. If the extractor is not available, it may be possible to use the method shown in the accompanying photograph. Wrap some emery cloth round the rotor and clamp onto the rotor two hose clips joined end to end. A two legged sprocket puller hooked onto the hose clips can then be used to pull off the rotor.
4   Disconnect the green/red striped wire from the neutral indicator switch.
5   Remove the two countersunk crosshead screws holding the stator plate to the crankcase and remove the stator plate complete with wires. If scribe marks are made across the stator plate and its housing, this will aid reassembly and may obviate the need to retime the ignition.
6   Remove the Woodruff key from the crankshaft, and collect the two small O-rings that seal the stator plate screws.

C90 model only

7   Remove the two screws and the final drive sprocket cover. This allows the eight screws and the generator cover to be removed.
8   Disconnect the green/red striped wire from the neutral indicator contact and remove the complete stator coil assembly from the left-hand crankcase by unscrewing the crosshead screws.
9   Hold the rotor stationary and remove the centre retaining bolt and washer.
10 Use a Honda extractor tool to remove the rotor. If the correct service tool extractor is not available, use a sprocket puller on a bolt screwed part way into the end of the crankshaft.

8 Cylinder head and cylinder: removal

Engine in the frame

As stated in Section 2 of this Chapter, it is possible to remove the cylinder head and the cylinder barrel whilst the engine is still in the frame. Only paragraphs 1 to 7 of Section 5 need to be completed before proceeding with the following dismantling procedure:

Engine removed from the frame

If the whole of Section 5 has been completed continue with the following dismantling procedure:

C50 and C70 models only

1   Remove the spark plug cap and unscrew the spark plug.
2   Remove the long bolt which passes through the centre of the camshaft and pull off the circular side cover on the left-hand side of the cylinder head.
3   Rotate the engine until the 'O' mark on the camshaft sprocket lines up with the notch on the cylinder head. This ensures that the engine is at top dead centre (TDC) on the compression stroke.
4   Remove the sealing plug and the camchain tensioner spring from the underside of the engine.
5   Remove the three bolts and the camshaft sprocket from the end of the camshaft.
6   Remove the four nuts and washers from the top of the engine, noting the position of the domed nuts and sealing washers. The top engine cover will now lift clear.
7   Remove the single bolt on the left-hand side of the engine and slide the cylinder head up the holding down studs, allowing the camshaft sprocket to drop clear of the cylinder head.
8   Remove the sprocket from the chain and remove the cylinder head gasket and its associated 'O' rings.
9   Remove the bearing bolt for the camchain guide roller and pull the roller clear.
10 Remove the single bolt on the left-hand side of the engine and

8.4 Remove the tensioner spring

8.5 Remove the three camshaft bolts

8.6 Remove the nuts and top cover

8.7 Slide the cylinder head up the studs

8.8 Remove the camshaft sprocket

8.10 Pad the crankcase mouth and slide off the barrel

Fig. 1.1. Cylinder head covers - C70 model

1	Top cover	6	Right-hand cover gasket
2	Right-hand cover	7	Left-hand cover gasket
3	Left-hand cover	8	Insulator block gasket
4	Tappet cover (2 off)	9	Insulator block
5	Top cover gasket	10	Washer (3 off)

11	Washer (2 off)	16	Dome nut (3 off)
12	O-ring (2 off)	17	Washer (2 off)
13	Bolt	18	Spark plug
14	Screw (2 off)		
15	Nut (3 off)		

Fig. 1.2. Cylinder head and barrel - C70 model

1	Inlet valve guide	5	Cylinder head assembly	9	Rubber seal (2 off)	13 Stud (2 off)
2	Exhaust valve guide	6	Cylinder head gasket	10	O-ring (2 off)	14 Screw
3	Cylinder barrel	7	Clip	11	Rubber seal	15 Dowel (2 off)
4	Cylinder base gasket	8	Bolt (2 off)	12	Stud (2 off)	16 Dowel (2 off)

Fig. 1.3. Cylinder head and barrel - C90 model

1 Cylinder barrel	10 Right-hand cover gasket	19 Gasket (2 off)	28 Dome nut
2 Cylinder base gasket	11 Camchain tunnel gasket	20 Clip	29 Dowel (2 off)
3 Cylinder head	12 Camchain tunnel gasket	21 Washer	30 Dowel
4 Cylinder head gasket	13 Insulator block gasket	22 Washer (3 off)	31 Screw
5 Gasket	14 Insulator block	23 O-ring (2 off)	32 Screw (3 off)
6 Top cover	15 Insulator block	24 Bolt (2 off)	33 Spark plug
7 Right-hand cover	16 Clip	25 Stud (2 off)	
8 Tappet cover (2 off)	17 Clip	26 Nut (2 off)	
9 Top cover gasket	18 Inlet pipe	27 Nut (3 off)	

slide the cylinder barrel up the holding down studs sufficiently to enable the crankcase mouth to be padded with a clean rag to stop any broken pieces or dirt falling inside the engine which would necessitate further engine dismantling to remove them. Slide the cylinder barrel further up the studs and support the piston as it falls clear of the barrel. Remove the barrel completely followed by the cylinder base gasket and 'O' ring.

C90 model only

The contact breaker assembly of this model is located within the cylinder head casting, where it is driven from an extension of the overhead camshaft. In consequence, a special dismantling procedure is necessary, as follows:

11 Remove the circular contact breaker cover on the cylinder head, held by two crosshead screws.

12 Disconnect the lead wire to the contact breaker assembly and remove the contact breaker assembly complete with back plate. It is retained in position by two crosshead screws, which should be removed. If the exact position of the back plate is marked with a scribe line in relation to its housing, this will aid reassembly and possibly obviate the need to retime the ignition.

13 Remove the automatic advance unit by withdrawing the hexagon head bolt from the centre of the camshaft. Remove also the dowel pin, which is used to ensure the assembly is replaced in the correct position.

14 Detach the contact breaker outer casting and gasket, which is held to the cylinder head casting by three crosshead screws.

15 Remove the spark plug cap and unscrew the spark plug.

16 Rotate the engine until the 'O' mark on the camshaft sprocket lines up with the notch on the cylinder head. This ensures that the engine is at top dead centre (TDC) on the compression stroke.

17 Remove the sealing plug and the camchain tensioner spring from the underside of the engine.

18 Remove the two bolts and pull the camshaft clear of the head leaving the chain and sprocket within the cylinder head.

19 Remove the four nuts and washers from the top of the engine, noting the positions of the domed nuts and sealing washers. The top engine cover will now lift clear.

20 Slide the cylinder head up the holding down studs, allowing the camshaft sprocket to drop clear of the cylinder head.

21 Remove the sprocket from the chain and remove the cylinder head gasket, the oil feed seal and the camchain tunnel seal.

22 Remove the bearing bolt for the camchain guide roller and pull the roller clear.

23 Slide the cylinder barrel up the holding down studs sufficiently to enable the crankcase mouth to be padded with a clean rag, to stop any broken pieces or dirt falling inside the engine which would necessitate further engine dismantling to remove them. Slide the cylinder barrel further up the studs and support the piston as it falls clear of the barrel. Remove the barrel completely followed by the cylinder base gasket and the camchain tunnel seal.

24 If the flywheel generator has been removed, the camchain can then be detached.

9 Piston and piston rings: removal

1 The gudgeon pin is of the fully floating type, retained by two wire circlips in the piston bosses. After the circlips have been removed, using pointed nose pliers, the pin can be tapped lightly from the piston.

2 Note the piston is marked with an arrow and must be positioned so that the arrow points downwards. If the piston is oversize, the amount will be stamped on the piston crown.

3 Remove the piston rings by expanding them gently, using extreme care because they are very brittle. If they prove difficult to remove, slide strips of tin behind them, to help ease them from their grooves. The top piston ring is of the chrome type and should have the mark 'top' on the uppermost face. The second ring is tapered and should have the 'top' mark in a similar position. A slotted oil scraper ring is fitted in the lower groove,

9.2 The piston is marked with an arrow

10.2a Use a bolt to withdraw the rocker pins ...

10.2b ... to release the rocker arms

which can be located with either face uppermost.

11.3a Remove the spring register ...

10 Camshaft and rocker arms: removal

1   The camshaft on the C50 and C70 models slides out of the cylinder head once the cam lobes have been lined up with their respective cutouts. The C90 model camshaft will have been removed in the cylinder head removal sequence.
2   Remove the two or three (C90 model) screws and the right-hand (finned) cover. Pull out the rocker pins by using a standard bolt screwed into the extraction thread. The engine mounting bolt is of the correct thread size. The rocker arms will now pull clear.

11 Valves and valve guides: removal

1   Remove the two tappet covers from the cylinder head.
2   Use a small size valve spring compressor to compress the springs and release the two half collets.
3   Release the valve spring compressor and remove the top spring register, the inner and outer valve springs, and on the exhaust valve only, the bottom spring register, the oil seal cover and the oil seal.
4   The valve will slide out of its guide. The other valve can now be treated in exactly the same way.
5   If it is necessary to remove the valve guides, they can be tapped out with a hammer and drift. Warming the cylinder head will help, as the guides are a tight fit.

11.3b ... the inner and outer valve springs ...

12 Oil filters: removal

1   As cleaning the oil filters is part of the routine maintenance the following procedure applies when at least paragraphs 1 to 5 of Section 5 have been completed.
2   Remove the kickstart bolt and pull the kickstart lever clear.
3   Ensure that there is no oil in the engine before removing the eight (C50 and C70 models) or nine screws (C90 model) and the right-hand cover. A deluge of oil will result if this simple precaution is not taken.

11.3c ... and the oil seal and cap

11.5 The valve guide will press out of the head

Fig. 1.4. Camshaft and valves - C70 model

1	Camshaft	5	Exhaust valve	9	Inner valve spring (2 off)	13	Tappet screw (2 off)
2	Rocker arm (2 off)	6	Oil seal	10	Spring retainer (2 off)	14	Tappet nut (2 off)
3	Rocker shaft (2 off)	7	Seal cover	11	Spring register		
4	Inlet valve	8	Outer valve spring (2 off)	12	Collet (4 off)		

Fig. 1.5. Camshaft and valves - C90 model

1 Inlet valve guide	6 Inlet valve	11 Inner valve spring (2 off)	16 Dowel
2 Exhaust valve guide	7 Exhaust valve	12 Spring retainer (2 off)	17 Tappet screw (2 off)
3 Camshaft	8 Oil seal	13 Spring register (2 off)	18 Tappet nut (2 off)
4 Rocker arm (2 off)	9 Seal cover	14 Spring register	19 O-ring (2 off)
5 Rocker shaft (2 off)	10 Outer valve spring (2 off)	15 Collet (4 off)	

12.4a Remove the clutch operating arm ...

12.4b ... and prise out the camplate

12.5 Remove the clutch outer plate to clean the filter

4   When the cover has been removed, it is probable that an anti-rattle spring will have dropped out of position. This is located between the clutch operating cam plate and the release mechanism, to eliminate chatter. Remove the washer (C50 model only) and the clutch operating lever from its splined shaft, lift off the ball bearing carrier and prise free the camplate from the centre of the clutch.

5   Remove the two (C90 model) or three (C50 and C70 models) screws that retain the clutch outer plate. This is also the centrifugal filter which may have an amount of dirt inside, so care should be taken when removing the plate to ensure that the dirt does not fall into the engine.

6   The filter gauze is located at the bottom of the engine, in a slot probably hidden by the old gasket.

13 Clutch and primary drive: removal

1   As stated in Section 2 of this Chapter, the clutch and primary drive can be removed whilst the engine is still in the frame but Section 12 must be completed first.

2   A special tool is now needed, preferably the Honda service tool, but a suitable equivalent can be made from a piece of tube. The tube is cut to leave two prongs which fit the special sleeve nut, as shown in the accompanying sketch.

Fig. 1.6. Clutch sleeve tool

1   Holes for tommy bar
2   Two pegs to engage with sleeve nut
3   Sleeve nut

13.3 Remove the sleeve nut

3   Prise out the tab washer, hold the clutch securely and use the special tool to remove the clutch centre nut.
4   The clutch will lift off as a unit and if further work on the clutch is necessary, Chapter 2 will provide all the information required.
5   Slide off from the crankshaft the primary drive pinion, the pinion bearing and the double diameter spacer.
6   Remove the circlip and slide the large primary drive pinion off its shaft.

14 Gearchange mechanism: removal

1   Remove the shouldered bolt and the index arm, with the spring still attached.
2   Remove the bolt in the gearchange drum, Remove the index plate and the four operating pins.
3   The gearchange spindle assembly will now pull clear, provided that the gearchange lever has already been removed.
4   Care should be taken to see that the springs do not fall off and are lost on the floor.

13.4 The clutch lifts off as a complete assembly

13.5a Remove the primary drive pinion ...

13.5b ... the centre bush ...

13.5c ... and the double diameter spacer

13.6a Remove the circlip ...

13.6b ... and slide the gear off its splines

14.1 Remove the pivot bolt and index arm

14.2a Remove the index plate ...

14.2b ... and the four pins

14.3 Slide out the gearchange mechanism

Fig. 1.7. Kickstart and gearchange - C70 model

1	Gearchange spindle assembly	5	Return spring	9	Spindle	13	Washer
2	Gearchange spindle	6	Spring stop	10	Spring retainer	14	Circlip
3	Gearchange arm	7	Pinion	11	Return spring	15	Circlip (2 off)
4	Arm spring	8	Ratchet spring	12	Washer	16	Circlip

OLD TYPE

Fig. 1.8. Kickstart and gearchange - C90 model

1	Index arm	10	Pawl
2	Index arm spring	11	Ratchet spring
3	Gearchange spindle	12	Guide
4	Gearchange arm	13	Spindle assembly
5	Arm spring	14	Return spring
6	Return spring	15	Bolt
7	Spring stop	16	Washer (2 off)
8	Pinion	17	Washer
9	Pawl spring		

15.1a Release the circlip ...

15.1b ... and slide off the spring and retainer

16.1b ... and lift the sprocket clear

15 Kickstart return spring: removal

C50 and C70 models only

1   Remove the circlip on the kickstart shaft and ease the spring retainer up the shaft whilst releasing the spring from the crankcase. Slide the spring and retainer off the shaft.

16 Final drive sprocket: removal

If the left-hand side cover and the final drive chain have been removed, the sprocket is released by removing the two bolts and the locking plate and pulling the sprocket off its splined shaft.

17 Crankcases: separating

1   If all the necessary components have been removed from the engine as previously described there are only eight screws holding the crankcases together and once these have been removed the right-hand crankcase should lift off with light tapping on the end of the crankshaft and gearshift.

16.1a Remove the bolts and the locking plate ...

17.1 After removing the screws lift the crankcase half clear

Fig. 1.9. Crankcases - C70 model

1	Right-hand crankcase assembly	
2	Right-hand crankcase assembly	
3	Crankcase gasket	
4	Left-hand crankcase assembly	
5	Left-hand crankcase assembly	
6	Oil filter	
7	Clip	
8	Stud (2 off)	
9	Stud (2 off)	
10	Sealing washer	
11	Dowel (2 off)	
12	Drain plug	
13	Screw	
14	Screw (3 off)	
15	Screw (4 off)	
16	Dowel (2 off)	

Fig. 1.10. Crankshaft and piston - C70 model

1	Crankshaft assembly	6	Circlip (2 off)	11	Left-hand crankshaft	16 Woodruff key
2	Crankshaft assembly	7	Connecting rod	12	Crank pin	17 Ball bearing (2 off)
3	Piston ring set	8	Roller cage	13	Sprocket	18 Big-end roller (22 off)
4	Piston	9	Right-hand crankshaft	14	Spacer	
5	Gudgeon pin	10	Left-hand crankshaft	15	Woodruff key	

Fig. 1.11. Gearchange drum - C70 model

1	Selector fork	11	Switch assembly
2	Selector fork	12	Switch contact
3	Selector fork pin (2 off)	13	Retaining plate
4	Pin clip (2 off)	14	O-ring
5	Gearchange drum	15	Pivot bolt
6	Gearchange drum	16	Washer
7	Index plate	17	Rubber plug
8	Index pin (4 off)	18	Bolt
9	Index arm	19	Screw
10	Arm spring	20	Screw

18.1 Remove the crankshaft assembly

18.2 Ensure that the camchain has been removed

19.1 Remove the kickstart shaft

2   Never use the point of a screwdriver to aid the separation of the crankcases. It will cause irreparable damage to the jointing surfaces.
3   There is no need to remove either the oil pump located behind the clutch or the camshaft chain tensioner assembly found at the rear of the flywheel generator. Neither impede the separation of the crankcases.

18 Crankshaft assembly: removal

1   The crankcase bearings are a sliding fit in the steel inserted housings in the crankcase. The crankshaft assembly, complete with bearings, should withdraw from the left-hand case without difficulty, using only light pressure.
2   Note that the camshaft chain will need to be pulled clear of the sprocket on the crankshaft before the crankshaft can be withdrawn.
3   Although it is possible to use an extractor to remove the crankshaft bearings it should be remembered that if the main bearings need replacing the big-end cannot be in the best of condition and a replacement crankshaft assembly is the safest course of action. Note that the cam chain sprocket will need to be removed before the left-hand bearing can be extracted.

19 Kickstart shaft assembly: removal

1   On the C50 and C70 models the kickstart shaft assembly will lift straight out of the crankcase half.
2   On the C90 model, the kickstarter return spring must be unhooked from the crankcase before the kickstart shaft assembly will lift out of the crankcase half. Remove the kickstart return spring.

20 Gear selector drum and gear cluster: removal

1   Remove the rubber blanking plug located at the side of the neutral indicator switch.
2   Remove the 10 mm bolt and washer retaining the gear selector drum in the crankcase (situated adjacent to the neutral indicator). The selector drum can now be withdrawn from the crankcase, together with the selectors and the gear cluster complete.
3   Care should be taken to avoid losing any shims or washers from the ends of the shafts.

21 Neutral indicator switch: removal

1   The neutral indicator switch is retained in position with a metal clamp and a single screw.
2   Remove the screw and clamp and slide the switch out of the crankcase half, taking care not to damage the sealing 'O' ring.

22 Camchain tensioner pulley and oil pump drive: removal

1   To remove the oil pump drive sprocket, hold the sprocket securely and unscrew the oil pump drive shaft. The sprocket can then be pulled clear but a note should be made regarding which way round it is fitted. The C90 model has a one-piece shaft and sprocket.
2   The tensioner ring on the C90 model with the tensioner pulley will lift off once the three bolts and retaining plates have been removed.
3   The tensioner arm on the C50 and C70 models pivots on a single shouldered bolt and removal of this bolt releases the arm.
4   The tensioner push rod if still in the crankcase half can now be pushed out.

20.1 Remove the bolt hidden under the rubber plug

20.2 Remove the gearbox components together

21.1 A screw and plate retain the neutral switch

22.1 Unscrew the oil pump driveshaft

22.3 Remove the pivot bolt and tensioner arm

22.4 Ensure the tensioner pushrod is pulled out

Fig. 1.12a. Gearbox components - C50 and C70 models

1	Mainshaft	6	Layshaft second gear	11	Bush
2	Layshaft	7	Mainshaft top gear	12	Washer
3	Layshaft low gear	8	Layshaft top gear	13	Washer
4	Mainshaft second gear	9	Sprocket	14	Splined washer (3 off)
5	Layshaft second gear	10	Retaining plate	15	Circlip (4 off)

16	Oil seal
17	Bolt (2 off)
18	Ball bearing (2 off)

Fig. 1.12b. Gearbox components - C90 model

1	Mainshaft	5	Layshaft second gear	9	Retaining plate	13	Circlip
2	Layshaft	6	Mainshaft top gear	10	Selector dog	14	Bolt
3	Layshaft low gear	7	Layshaft top gear	11	Thrust washer	15	Ball bearing
4	Mainshaft second gear	8	Sprocket	12	Spline washer	16	Ball bearing

24.1 Check the condition of the oil seals

25.2 The bearings are a drive fit in the crankcases

27.2 Check the crankshaft assembly for wear

23 Oil pump: removal

1   Remove the three large screws and the oil pump assembly complete will lift clear of the right-hand crankcase.
2   The oil pump and the lubrication system are dealt with in Chapter 3 which includes all the necessary information on oil pump operation and renovation.

24 Oil seals: removal

1   Two oil seals are fitted in the left-hand crankcase, located at the gearbox layshaft bearing and gear lever shaft on the C50 and C70 models, whilst the C90 model has the gear lever shaft oil seal in the generator cover. There is also an oil seal on the kickstart shaft bearing in the clutch cover.
2   The oil seals are easily removed by prising them out of position with a screwdriver. Care should be taken to ensure the lip of the bearing housing is not damaged during this operation.

25 Crankshaft and gearbox main bearings: removal

1   The crankshaft bearings will remain on their shafts when the crankshaft assembly is withdrawn from the crankcase. A puller or an extractor will be necessary for their removal as they are a tight fit.
2   The gearbox bearings are a light press fit in the crankcase castings. They can be drifted out of position, using a mandrel of the correct size and a hammer.
3   If necessary, warm the crankcases slightly, to aid the release of the bearings.

26 Examination and renovation: general

1   Before examining the parts of the dismantled engine unit for wear, it is essential that they should be cleaned thoroughly. Use a paraffin/petrol mix to remove all traces of old oil and sludge that may have accumulated within the engine.
2   Examine the crankcase castings for cracks or other signs of damage. If a crack is discovered, it will require professional repair.
3   Examine carefully each part to determine the extent of wear, if necessary checking with the tolerance figures listed in the Specifications section of this Chapter.
4   Use a clean, lint-free rag for cleaning and drying the various components, otherwise there is risk of small particles obstructing the internal oilways.

27 Big-end and main bearings: examination and renovation

1   Failure of the big-end is invariably accompanied by a knock from within the crankcase that progressively becomes worse. Some vibration will also be experienced. There should be no vertical play in the big-end bearing after the old oil has been washed out. If even a small amount of play is evident, the bearing is due for replacement. Do not run the machine with a worn big-end bearing, otherwise there is risk of breaking the connecting rod or crankshaft.
2   It is not possible to separate the flywheel assembly in order to replace the bearing because the parallel sided crankpin is pressed into the flywheels. Big-end repair should be entrusted to a Honda agent, who will have the necessary repair or replacement facilities.
3   Failure of the main bearings is usually evident in the form of an audible rumble from the bottom end of the engine, accompanied by vibration. The vibration will be most noticeable through the footrests.
4   The crankshaft main bearings are of the journal ball type. If wear is evident in the form of play or if the bearings feel rough

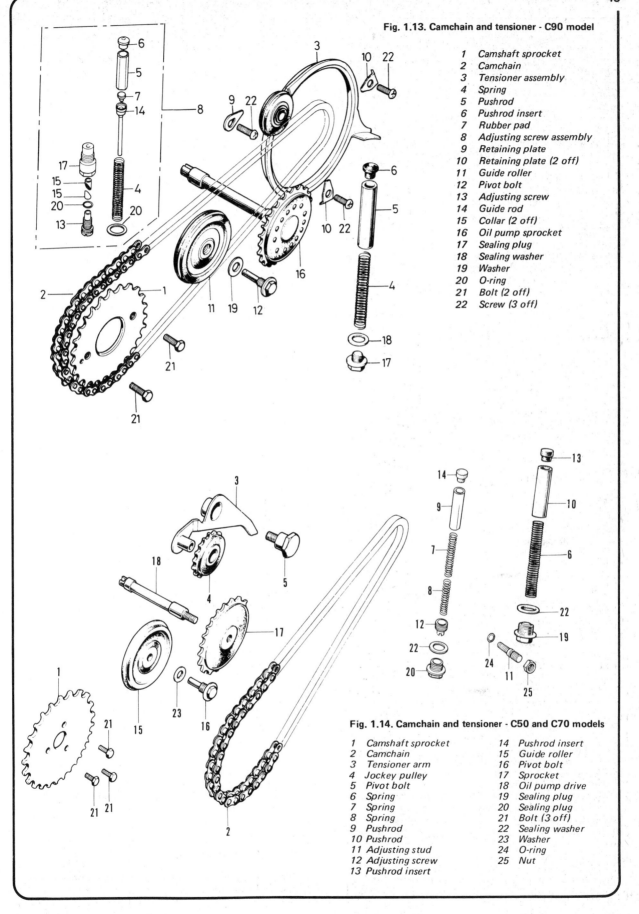

Fig. 1.13. Camchain and tensioner - C90 model

1 Camshaft sprocket
2 Camchain
3 Tensioner assembly
4 Spring
5 Pushrod
6 Pushrod insert
7 Rubber pad
8 Adjusting screw assembly
9 Retaining plate
10 Retaining plate (2 off)
11 Guide roller
12 Pivot bolt
13 Adjusting screw
14 Guide rod
15 Collar (2 off)
16 Oil pump sprocket
17 Sealing plug
18 Sealing washer
19 Washer
20 O-ring
21 Bolt (2 off)
22 Screw (3 off)

Fig. 1.14. Camchain and tensioner - C50 and C70 models

1 Camshaft sprocket
2 Camchain
3 Tensioner arm
4 Jockey pulley
5 Pivot bolt
6 Spring
7 Spring
8 Spring
9 Pushrod
10 Pushrod
11 Adjusting stud
12 Adjusting screw
13 Pushrod insert
14 Pushrod insert
15 Guide roller
16 Pivot bolt
17 Sprocket
18 Oil pump drive
19 Sealing plug
20 Sealing plug
21 Bolt (3 off)
22 Sealing washer
23 Washer
24 O-ring
25 Nut

as they are rotated, replacement is necessary. To remove the main bearings, if the appropriate service tool is not available, insert two thin steel wedges, one on each side of the bearing, and with these clamped in a vice hit the end of the crankshaft squarely with a rawhide mallet in an attempt to drive the crankshaft through the bearing. When the bearing has moved the initial amount, it should be possible to insert a conventional two or three legged sprocket puller, to complete the drawing-off action.

5　Note that the bottom camshaft chain sprocket must be withdrawn from the left-hand crankshaft before access can be gained to the main bearing. The sprocket is recessed to accommodate a puller.

6　The small end eye should also be checked for wear as the gudgeon pin should be a good fit. The piston should pivot on the gudgeon pin rather than the gudgeon pin rotate in the connecting rod.

28 Cylinder barrel: examination and renovation

1　The usual indications of a badly worn cylinder barrel and piston are excessive oil consumption and piston slap, a metallic rattle that occurs when there is little or no load on the engine. If the top of the bore of the cylinder barrel is examined carefully, it will be found that there is a ridge on the thrust side, the depth of which will vary according to the amount of wear that has taken place. This marks the limit of travel of the uppermost piston ring.

2　Measure the bore diameter just below the ridge, using an internal micrometer. Compare this reading with the diameter at the bottom of the cylinder bore, which has not been subject to wear. If the difference in readings exceeds 0.005 inch it is necessary to have the cylinder rebored and to fit an oversize piston and rings.

3　If an internal micrometer is not available, the amount of cylinder bore wear can be measured by inserting the piston without rings so that it is approximately ¾ inch from the top of the bore. If it is possible to insert 0.004 inch feeler gauge between the piston and the cylinder wall on the thrust side of the piston, remedial action must be taken.

4　Check the surface of the cylinder bore for score marks or any other damage that may have resulted from an earlier engine seizure or displacement of the gudgeon pin. A rebore will be necessary to remove any deep indentations, irrespective of the amount of bore wear, otherwise a compression leak will occur.

5　Check that the external cooling fins are not clogged with oil or road dirt; otherwise the engine will overheat. When clean, a coating of matt cylinder black will help improve the heat radiation.

29 Piston and piston rings: examination and renovation

1　If a rebore is necessary, the existing piston and rings can be disregarded because they will be replaced with their oversize equivalents as a matter of course.

2　Remove all traces of carbon from the piston crown, using a soft scraper to ensure the surface is not marked. Finish off by polishing the crown, with metal polish, so that carbon does not adhere so easily in the future. Never use emery cloth.

3　Piston wear usually occurs at the skirt or lower end of the piston and takes the form of vertical streaks or score marks on the thrust side. There may also be some variation in the thickness of the skirt.

4　The piston ring grooves may also become enlarged in use, allowing the piston rings to have greater side float. If the clearance exceeds 0.004 inch for the two compression rings, or 0.005 inch for the oil control ring, the piston is due for replacement. It is unusual for this amount of wear to occur on its own.

5　Piston ring wear is measured by removing the rings from the piston and inserting them in the cylinder bore using the crown of the piston to locate them approximately 1½ inches from the top of the bore. Make sure they rest square with the bore. Measure

the end gap with a feeler gauge; if the gap exceeds 0.010 inch they require replacement, assuming the cylinder barrel is not in need of a rebore.

30 Valves, valve seats and valve guides: examination and renovation

1　After cleaning the valves to remove all traces of carbon, examine the heads for signs of pitting and burning. Examine also the valve seats in the cylinder head. The exhaust valve and its seat will probably require the most attention because these are the hotter running of the two. If the pitting is slight, the marks can be removed by grinding the seats and valves together using fine valve grinding compound.

2　Valve grinding is a simple task, carried out as follows. Smear a trace of fine valve grinding compound (carborundum paste) on the seat face and apply a suction grinding tool to the head of the valve. With a semi-rotary motion, grind in the valve head to its seat, using a backward and forward action. It is advisable to lift the valve occasionally, to distribute the grinding compound evenly. Repeat this operation until an unbroken ring of light grey matt finish is obtained on both valve and seat. This denotes the grinding operation is complete. Before passing to the next operation, make quite sure that all traces of the grinding compound have been removed from both the valve and its seat and that none has entered the valve guide. If this precaution is not observed, rapid wear will take place, due to the abrasive nature of the carborundum base.

3　When deeper pit marks are encountered, it will be necessary to use a valve refacing machine and also a valve seat cutter, set to an angle of 45°. Never resort to excessive grinding because this will only pocket the valve and lead to reduced engine efficiency. If there is any doubt about the condition of a valve, fit a new replacement.

4　Examine the condition of the valve collets and the groove on the valve in which they seat. If there is any sign of damage, new replacements should be fitted. If the collets work loose whilst the engine is running, a valve will drop in and cause extensive damage.

5　Measure the valve stems for wear, making reference to the tolerance values given in the Specifications section of this Chapter. Check also the valve guides, which can be removed by heating the cylinder head in an oven then using a two diameter drift to drive them out of position. The initial diameter of the drift must be a good fit in the valve guide stem. Replace with the new valve guides whilst the cylinder head is still warm.

6　Check the free length of the valve springs against the list of tolerance in the Specifications. If the springs are reduced in length or if there is any doubt about their condition, they should be replaced.

31 Cylinder head: decarbonisation and examination

1　Remove all traces of carbon from the cylinder head and valve ports, using a soft scraper. Extreme care should be taken to ensure the combustion chamber and valve seats are not marked in any way, otherwise hot spots and leakages may occur. Finish by polishing the combustion chamber so that carbon does not adhere so easily in the future. Use metal polish and NOT emery cloth.

2　Check to make sure that valve guides are free from carbon or any other foreign matter that may cause the valves to stick.

3　Make sure the cylinder head fins are not clogged with oil or road dirt, otherwise the engine will overheat. If necessary, use a wire brush.

32 Camshaft, rockers and rocker shafts: examination

1　The cams should have a smooth surface and be free from scuff marks or indentations. It is unlikely that severe wear will be encountered during the normal service life of the machine unless the lubrication system has failed or the case hardened surface has broken through.

2   Check the oil groove on the end of the camshaft to ensure it is clean and free from sludge.

3   The internal oilways in the camshaft should also be cleaned and blown through to remove any obstruction.

4   It is unlikely that excessive wear will occur in the rocker arms and rocker shafts, but if it does it will be for the same reasons. A clicking noise from the rocker box is the usual symptom of wear in the rocker components, which should not be confused with the noise that results from excessive tappet clearance. If any shake is present and the rocker arm is loose on its shaft, a new rocker and/or shaft should be fitted.

5   Check the tip of the rocker arm at the point where it bears on the camshaft. If signs of cracking, scuffing or breakthrough are found in the case hardened surface, fit a new replacement. Check also the condition of the thread on the tappet, the rocker arm and the locknut.

33 Camshaft chain tensioner and sprockets: examination

1   An oil damped camshaft chain tensioner is employed, to fulfill the dual function of controlling the chain tension at high engine speeds and eliminating mechanical noise. A compression spring and pushrod within a guide provides the tension by bearing on one end of a pivoting arm which carries a jockey pulley on the other. The jockey pulley engages with the top run of the chain. The guide containing the spring and pushrod floods with oil when the engine is running, to provide the necessary damping medium.

2   The chain tensioner spring should have a free length of 3.04 inches. It should be replaced if the free length is reduced below 2.89 inches. To gain access to the spring and pushrod assembly, remove the 14 mm bolt that screws at an angle into the base of the left-hand crankcase.

3   Adjustment of the tensioner is automatic. Check that the tensioner is operating correctly when the left-hand flywheel generator cover and flywheel generator are removed.

4   The camshaft is of the endless variety and should not contain a split link.

5   It is unlikely that the camchain sprockets will need renewing unless the teeth have been damaged or broken.

6   Clean the sprockets so that any timing marks are easily identified.

7   It should be noted that later models may have a manual type of tensioner fitted. Refer to the Routine Maintenance Chapter for information on how to recognise and adjust this type of tensioner.

34 Gearchange mechanism: examination

1   Examine the mechanism for any signs of damage, renewing any of the springs which may have become weak or broken.

2   Check for wear on the gearchange lever pawls as this can cause missed gearchanges.

35 Kickstart assembly: examination

1   Give the kickstart assembly a close visual inspection for signs of wear or damage such as broken or chipped teeth, removing the necessary circlips if dismantling for renewal of any parts.

2   Examine the kickstart return spring for weakness or damage. This component is often overlooked, even though it is tensioned every time the kickstart is depressed. It is best to renew as a precaution during a major overhaul, to prevent a further stripdown later.

36 Primary drive gears: examination

Both primary drive gears should be examined closely to ensure that there is no damage to the teeth. The depth of mesh is predetermined by the bearing locations and cannot be adjusted.

37 Gear selector drum and gear cluster: examination

1   This group of components was removed from the crankshaft as a unit, with care being taken to avoid losing any shims or washers from the ends of the shafts. The parts fall naturally into three sub-assemblies; the selector drum, the mainshaft and the layshaft.

2   The selector drum sub-assembly should be examined to ensure that the selector forks will slide easily on the drum without too much play. Check that the selector forks are not bent or excessively worn. To renew either selector fork, remove the spring clip and the cam track follower and slide the selector fork clear. When reassembling, ensure that the selector fork is fitted the right way round.

3   The mainshaft and layshaft sub-assemblies should be examined closely for any signs of wear or damage such as

33.5 Check the sprocket for worn or broken teeth

35.1 Check the condition of the ratchet spring

37.1 Note the relative positions before dismantling the gearbox components

37.2 Check the selector forks for wear or damage

37.3a Check for wear on the layshaft components ...

37.3b ... and the mainshaft components ...

37.3c ... and ensure the circlips are properly seated on reassembly

broken or chipped teeth, worn dogs and damaged or worn splines. Renew any parts found unserviceable as they cannot be reclaimed. To renew any parts, removal of the circlips, washers and gears until the defective part is reached is straightforward and if the parts are laid out in sequence, reassembly should present no problems.

38 Engine reassembly: general

1   Before reassembly is commenced, the various engine and gearbox components should be thoroughly clean and placed close to the working area.

2   Make sure all traces of the old gaskets have been removed and the mating surfaces are clean and undamaged. One of the best ways to remove old gasket cement is to apply a rag soaked in methylated spirit. This acts as a solvent and will ensure the cement is removed without resort to scraping and the consequent risk of damage.

3   Gather together all the necessary tools and have available an oil can filled with clean engine oil. Make sure all the new gaskets and oil seals are to hand; nothing is more frustrating than having to stop in the middle of a reassembly sequence because a vital gasket or replacement has been overlooked.

4   Make sure the reassembly area is clean and that there is adequate working space. Refer to the torque and clearance settings wherever they are given. Many of the smaller bolts are easily sheared if they are over-tightened. Always use the correct size screwdriver bit for the crosshead screws and never an ordinary screwdriver or punch.

39 Engine reassembly: fitting the bearings and oil seals to the crankcases and clutch cover

1   Before fitting any of the crankcase bearings make sure that the bearing housings are scrupulously clean and that there are no burrs or lips on the entry to the housings. Press or drive the bearings into the cases using a mandrel and hammer, after first making sure that they are lined up squarely. Warming the crankcases will help when a bearing is a particularly tight fit.
2   When the bearings have been driven home, lightly oil them and make sure they revolve smoothly. This is particularly important in the case of the main bearings.
3   Using a soft mandrel, drive the oil seals into their respective housings. Do not use more force than is necessary because the seals damage very easily.
4   Lightly oil all the other moving parts as a prelude to re-assembly. This will ensure all working parts are lubricated adequately during the initial start-up of the rebuilt engine.

40 Engine reassembly: refitting the oil pump

1   Reference to Chapter 3 will fully explain the operation and renovation of the oil pump so that it is ready to fit to the crankcase as a sub-assembly.
2   Smear a very thin film of jointing compound such as Golden Hermatite onto the crankcase face and stick the gasket in position. Do not use an excessive amount of jointing compound as serious engine damage can result if any of the oil-ways are blocked.
3   Fit the oil pump in position and secure it with three screws. Check that it is free to rotate.

41 Engine reassembly: refitting the camchain tensioner pulley and oil pump drive

1   On the C50 and C70 models, fit the tensioner arm and its shouldered pivot bolt.
2   On the C90 model, fit the tensioner ring and secure it in position with the three retaining plates and bolts.
3   Feed the oil pump drive sprocket into the crankcase ensuring that it fits the right way round, and screw in the drive shaft. Hold the sprocket securely and fully tighten the shaft.

42 Engine reassembly: refitting the neutral indicator switch

1   Ensure that the sealing 'O' ring on the neutral indicator switch is in good condition before pushing the switch into the crankcase.
2   Fit the switch retaining plate and screw.

43 Engine reassembly: replacing the gear selector drum and gear cluster

1   Place the left-hand crankcase on wooden blocks or an engine stand so that the inner side faces upwards.
2   Engage the selector forks in their respective positions, with the sliding dog on the layshaft and second gear on the mainshaft. Viewed endwise the lower of the two selector forks engages with the sliding dog on the layshaft and the upper fork with the sliding second gear pinion on the mainshaft.

41.1 Refit the tensioner arm and pivot bolt

41.3 Ensure that the sprocket is the right way round

42.1 Check that the O-ring is in good condition

43.3a Reassemble the gearbox cluster ...

3   Holding the complete gear assembly in the right-hand, locate the layshaft in the journal ball bearing, the mainshaft in the plain bush and the tapered end of the selector drum in its housing. The 10 mm bolt and washer that hold the selector drum can then be fitted into the underside of the crankcase half. Tighten this bolt and later fit the rubber blanking plug.

44 Engine reassembly: replacing the kickstart shaft assembly

1   The kickstart shaft will feed into the crankcase half but on the C90 model the kickstart return spring will need retensioning before the shaft will seat home properly.
2   Ensure that the kickstart friction spring is properly located in the crankcase half.

45 Engine reassembly: replacing the crankshaft assembly

1   Fit the crankshaft assembly in the left-hand crankcase with the splined mainshaft uppermost. Make sure the connecting rod clears the aperture for the cylinder barrel spigot. It may be

43.3b ... and retain the selector drum with this bolt

44.2 Refit the kickstart shaft with ratchet spring in cast groove

45.1 Refit the crankshaft assembly

46.3 Refit the crankcase half and ensure all the shafts still rotate

necessary to tap the assembly into position, if the crankshaft journal ball bearing is a tight fit in the steel outer ring.

46 Engine reassembly: rejoining the crankcases

1 Smear the joint face with Golden Hermatite or other jointing compound and stick the gasket to the crankcase joint.
2 Ensure that the crankcase dowels are in position.
3 Lower the other crankcase half into position. Gentle tapping may be required to fit the two halves together as the bearings and dowels are a tight fit.
4 Rotate all the shafts to ensure that they will turn and that no binding occurs, especially the oil pump drive shaft, to ensure that the slot engages with the oil pump.
5 Excessive force should not be used as this shows something has been wrongly assembled or is out of alignment.
6 Replace the eight screws which hold the crankcase together.

47 Engine reassembly: refitting the final drive sprocket

1 Now is an ideal time to fit the rubber blanking plug over the end of the gear selector drum.
2 The sprocket is pushed on the splines followed by the locking plate. The locking plate is turned in the groove and the two bolts tightened to clamp the plate to the sprocket.

48 Engine reassembly: replacing and tensioning the kickstart return spring (C50 and C70 models only)

1 Rotate the kickstart shaft clockwise until it will go no further.
2 Fit the spring and retainer onto the shaft and engage the splines by gently easing the shaft anti-clockwise to ensure that the spring retainer hits the return stop.
3 Wind the kickstart return spring round until it hooks into the crankcase. Refit the retaining circlip.

49 Engine reassembly: refitting the gearchange mechanism

1 Check the condition of the pawl spring and the return spring on the gearchange shaft assembly before assembling it into the crankcase.

47.1 Refit the rubber plug

47.2a Refit the sprocket ...

47.2b ... relocate the retaining plate ...

47.2c ... and tighten the two bolts

48.3 Replace the circlip to hold the spring retainer

49.1 Ensure the return spring fits round the spring stop

49.3a Refit the four pins ...

49.3b ... and retain them with the index plate

2   Grease the oil seal and carefully feed the gearchange shaft into position, ensuring that the splines do not damage the oil seal. An alternative method is to fit a small plastic bag over the shaft for feeding through the oil seal.
3   Refit the four small pins and the index plate onto the end of the gearchange drum, noting that the index plate is seated properly in the correct position.
4   Check the condition of the index arm spring and then refit the index arm with the shouldered bolt.

50 Engine reassembly: reassembling the clutch and primary drive

1   The large primary drive pinion is fitted on the splines of the mainshaft and retained with a circlip.
2   Fit the double diameter spacer, the pinion bearing and the small drive pinion onto the crankshaft.
3   Reference to Chapter 2 will fully explain the operation and renovation of the clutch, so that it is ready to fit the crankshaft as a sub-assembly.
4   Fit the clutch sub-assembly, the tab washer and the special nut to the crankshaft.
5   Hold the clutch securely and tighten the sleeve nut to a torque of 27.5 to 32.5 ft lb as recommended in the Specifications section of this Chapter. Prise the tab washer into one of the slots in the sleeve nut.

51 Engine reassembly: replacing the oil filters

1   Smear a thin film of jointing compound such as Golden Hermatite on the outer face of the clutch and stick the gasket into position.
2   Refit the clutch outer plate to form the centrifugal filter and retain it with two screws (on the C90 model) or three screws (C50 and C70 models).
3   Check that the orifice in the clutch camplate is clean and the pressure relief spring is in good condition.
4   Fit the orifice and spring into the camplate and fit the camplate into the clutch outer plate.
5   Position the anti-rattle spring and locate the ball bearing carrier onto the spring.
6   Refit the clutch operating arm onto its splines, ensuring that the arm points towards the centre of the clutch. The C50 model has an additional washer fitted on the shaft.

49.4 Refit the index arm and pivot bolt

50.1 Retain the gear with the circlip

50.2a Refit the double diameter spacer and the bush ...

50.2b ... and slide the gear pinion into position

50.4 Ensure the clutch is properly located on its splines and the primary drive pinion

50.5 Prise the tab washer into one of the slots when the nut is fully tightened

51.4 Refit the camplate and oil orifice

51.5 Fit the spring and the ball retainer

51.6 Refit the operating arm

51.7 Slide the filter gauze into its slot

52.2a Reassemble the valve ...

52.2b ... the oil seal ...

7 Slide the clean filter gauze each into its slot in the bottom of the crankcase.

8 Smear the joint face with Golden Hermatite or other jointing compound and stick the gasket to the crankcase. Ensure that the two dowels are fitted correctly.

9 Slacken the clutch adjustment stud and locknut and lower the clutch cover into position, ensuring that the ball bearing carrier is not disturbed.

10 Gentle tapping may be required to ensure that the cover is fully home on the dowels. Care should be taken to ensure that the oil seal on the kickstart shaft is not damaged.

11 Replace the eight screws (on the C50 and C70 models) or nine screws (C90 model) which hold the cover but do not fully tighten the screw that carries the spark plug lead clip.

12 Readjust the clutch release mechanism and tighten the locknut as described in Chapter 2.6.

13 The kickstart lever and bolt can be replaced at this stage, but it is customary to refit these components once the engine is in the frame.

52 Engine reassembly: replacing the valves and valve guides

1 When reassembling the valve guides into the cylinder head use a drift that fits the guide, such as the Honda service tool or use a long bolt and spacers and draw the guide into the head. It is possible to fractionally close the bore of a valve guide with hammering so that a valve will not slide freely - even though new parts have been used. Do not forget the 'O' ring seal.

2 The valve is fitted into the guide. The oil seal, oil seal cover and bottom spring register are fitted to the exhaust valve only, then the inner and outer valve springs and the spring register are clamped with a small valve spring compressor and the two half collets fitted. When removing the compressor ensure that the half collets are seating correctly.

3 The above procedure applies to both valves. The exhaust valve guide oil seal should be checked for damage if the engine has an oily exhaust.

53 Engine reassembly: replacing the camshaft and rocker arms

1 The camshaft of the C50 and C70 models slides into the cylinder head once the cam lobes are lined up with the cutouts in the cylinder head. The C90 model camshaft is fitted after the cylinder head is attached to the engine.

52.2c ... the oil seal cap ...

52.2d ... the inner and outer valve springs ...

52.2e ... the spring register ...

52.2f ... and retain it all with two collets

53.1 Line up the cam lobes with the cutaways in the head

2   Slacken the tappet adjusting screws, position each rocker arm and slide the rocker pin into place, ensuring that the extraction thread is outermost.

3   On the C50 and C70 models the tappet adjustment can be made now but the operation is described later in this Chapter, when the engine is in the frame.

54 Engine reassembly: refitting the piston and cylinder barrel

1   Raise the connecting rod to its highest point and pad the mouth of the crankcase with clean rag as a precaution against displaced parts falling into the crankcase.

2   Assemble the piston on the connecting rod, with the arrow on the piston crown facing downwards.

3   Lightly oil and fit the piston onto the connecting rod by inserting the gudgeon pin. Replace the circlips that retain the gudgeon pin making doubly sure that they are correctly seated in their grooves. Always renew the circlips as it is false economy to re-use the originals.

4   Thread the cam chain into position and ensure it seats properly onto the sprockets. Check that the two dowels are

53.2a Reposition the rocker arms ...

53.2b ... and slide the rocker pins into position

54.2 Refit the piston ensuring circlips are seated correctly

54.4 Thread the camshaft chain into position

properly located on the holding down studs.

5 The cylinder base gasket should be stuck in position with Golden Hermatite or other jointing compound, and the oil seal for the oil hole pushed into position.

6 The cylinder barrel should be fed onto the holding down studs. A piece of wire can be used to hook the cam chain through the cam chain tunnel.

7 The barrel should be lightly oiled and pushed further down the studs until the piston starts to enter the bore. The piston rings can then be compressed and fed into the bore.

8 When all three piston rings are in the bore the padding in the crankcase can be removed and the barrel slid down the studs to locate with the two dowels.

9 On the C50 and C70 models the cylinder barrel is retained in position by fitting the bolt on the left-hand side of the engine, finger tight.

10 Refit the guide roller into the camchain tunnel and retain it with the bearing bolt.

55 Engine reassembly: replacing the cylinder head and timing the valves (C50 and C70 models only)

1 Before the cylinder head can be fitted to the engine it must be fully assembled. Although it may appear possible to replace the rockers when the cylinder head is bolted down, this is not so in practice. The rocker spindles are retained by the long holding down studs that pass through the cylinder head and cannot be removed or replaced unless the cylinder head is lifted.

2 Refit the dowels on the holding down studs and fit a new cylinder head gasket and its associated 'O' ring for sealing the oil passageways.

3 To ease later assembly, ensure that the piston is at top dead centre (TDC) and the camshaft is also positioned such that the cam lobes point downward, the corresponding position to top dead centre on the compression stroke. Fit the camshaft sprocket into the camchain so that the 'O' mark is positioned at the top.

4 Lower the cylinder head onto the studs and feed the camshaft sprocket into the camchain tunnel. Locate the cylinder head on the two dowels and push the sprocket onto the spigot on the end of the camshaft.

5 Fit the holding down bolt on the left-hand side of the engine, finger tight.

6 Check that the engine is still at top dead centre and with the lower run of the camchain taut, that the 'O' mark on the

54.6 Slide the cylinder barrel down the studs

54.10 Refit the guide roller in the barrel

55.3 Fit a new gasket and seals and the sprocket

55.4a Slide the cylinder head down the studs ...

55.4b ... and fit the sprocket onto the camshaft

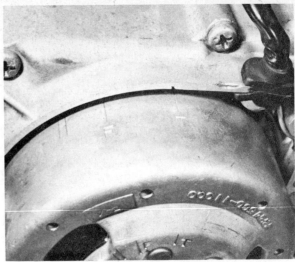
55.6a Line up the 'T' mark with the crankcase mark ...

55.6b ... and the 'O' mark with the cylinder head mark for correct valve timing

55.7a Reassemble the tensioner pushrod ...

55.7b ... and spring and refit the sealing plug

55.8a Refit the top cover ...

sprocket lines up with the notch on the cylinder head. The camshaft should be in the correct position for the three bolts to be fitted, retaining the sprocket.

7   Slide the camchain tensioner plunger and pressure spring into the crankcase and fit the sealing plug, after ensuring that the sealing washer is in good condition. Recheck the timing to ensure that it is correct.

8   The top cover gasket should be stuck in position with Golden Hermatite or other jointing compound and the top finned cover fitted, so that the arrow between the central fins points towards the exhaust valve.

9   Fit the nuts and washers ensuring that the domed nuts and sealing washers are fitted in their correct positions, and pull down evenly until the recommended torque settings are achieved (6.5 - 8.7 ft lb). Always tighten in a diagonal sequence, an essential requirement because an alloy cylinder head will distort easily. There is a separate bolt on the left-hand side of the cylinder head, just below the circular camshaft sprocket aperture, and below this, a bolt at the base of the cylinder barrel. Both must be tightened, as they are only finger tight at present.

10 Stick the side cover gaskets into position, again using Golden Hermatite, and bolt the finned cover then the circular cover into place. Refit the spark plug.

C90 model only

11 Before the cylinder head can be fitted to the engine, the rocker arms must be assembled. Although it may appear possible to replace the rockers when the cylinder head is bolted down, this is not so in practice. The rocker spindles are retained by the long holding down studs that pass through the cylinder head and cannot be removed or replaced unless the cylinder head is lifted.

12 Refit the dowels on the holding down studs and fit a new cylinder head gasket, oil feed seal and camchain tunnel seal.

13 To ease later assembling, ensure that the piston is at top dead centre (TDC) and fit the camshaft sprocket into the camchain so that the 'O' mark is positioned at the top.

14 Lower the cylinder head onto the studs and feed the camshaft sprocket into the camchain tunnel. Locate the cylinder head on the two dowels.

15 Feed the camshaft into the cylinder head through the sprocket and line the dowel pin up with 'O' mark, which should be in line with the notch on the cylinder head. Fit and finger tighten the two bolts securing the sprocket to the camshaft.

16 Slide the camchain tensioner plunger and pressure spring into the crankcase and fit the sealing plug, after ensuring that the

sealing washer is in good condition. Recheck the timing to ensure that it is correct.

17 The top cover gasket should be stuck in position with Golden Hermatite or other jointing compound and the top finned cover fitted so that the arrow between the central fins points towards the exhaust valve.

18 Fit the nuts and washers, ensuring that the domed nuts and sealing washers are fitted in their correct positions, and pull down evenly until the recommended torque settings are achieved (6.5 - 8.7 ft lb). Always tighten in a diagonal sequence, an essential requirement because an alloy cylinder head will distort easily.

19 Fully tighten the camshaft bolts.

20 Stick the side gaskets into position, again using Golden Hermatite, and bolt first the finned side cover then fix the contact breaker base into place with three screws. Ensure that the oil seal in the base is in good condition and undamaged.

21 Refit the dowel pin and the automatic advance mechanism and replace the bolt in the centre of the camshaft. Check the condition of the springs and the smooth action of the advance mechanism, renovating if necessary.

22 Refit the contact breaker assembly complete with the back plate and retain it with two screws, lining up with the scribe marks made inside during the dismantling stage. Reconnect the lead wire. If the contact breaker needs adjusting refer to Chapter 4 for full details. Always check the ignition timing, even if the scribe marks made earlier are in alignment with one another.

23 Stick the cover gasket into position again using Golden Hermatite and refit the cover and two screws. Refit the spark plug.

---

56 Engine reassembly: adjusting the tappets

1   The tappets should be adjusted to 0.002 inch clearance when the engine is cold and the piston is at top dead centre (TDC) on the compression stroke.

2   To adjust the tappets, slacken the locknut at the end of the rocker arm and turn the square-ended adjuster until the clearance is correct, as measured by a feeler gauge. Hold the square-ended adjuster firmly when the locknut is tightened, otherwise it will move and the adjustment will be lost.

3   After completing the adjustment to both valves, refit and tighten the rocker box caps, using new 'O' ring seals. Use a spanner that is a good fit otherwise the caps will damage easily.

55.8b ... with the arrow pointing towards the exhaust valve

55.10 Refit the side covers

56.3 Refit the tappet covers

57 Engine reassembly: replacing the flywheel generator

C50 and C70 models only

1   Fit the two small 'O' rings that seal the stator plate screws in their counterbores, and fit the Woodruff key into the crankshaft.

2   Ensure that the central oil seal and the large 'O' ring on the outside diameter of the stator plate are in good condition and undamaged before fitting the plate in position. Secure it with the two screws, aligning the scribe marks made when the stator plate was removed, and fit the rubber grommets on the wires into their respective cutouts.

3   Reconnect the green/red striped wire to the neutral indicator switch.

4   Before fitting the flywheel rotor, place a few drops of light oil on the felt wick which lubricates the contact breaker cam in the centre of the flywheel rotor.

5   It is advisable to check also whether the contact breaker points require attention at this stage, otherwise it will be necessary to withdraw the flywheel rotor again in order to gain access. Reference to Chapter 4, will show how the contact breaker points are renovated and adjusted.

57.1 Check that all the seals are in good condition

57.2 Refit the stator plate

57.8 Refit the rotor

58.2 Fit the spring link with the closed end facing the direction of chain travel

6   Check the condition of the springs and the smooth action of the automatic advance mechanism, renovating if necessary.
7   Feed the rotor onto the crankshaft so that the slot lines up with the Woodruff key. The rotor may have to be turned to clear the heel of the contact breaker before it will slide fully home.
8   The washer and rotor nut can now be fitted and the nut fully tightened, to the specified torque of 23.9 - 27.5 ft lb.
9   Refit the flywheel cover and secure it with three screws only if the engine is in the frame. Check the ignition timing, to verify it is correct.

C90 model only

1   Fit the rotor and secure it with its bolt and washer, tightening the bolt to the specified torque of 23.9 - 27.5 ft lb.
2   Fit the stator coils and secure them with the two screws, and fit the rubber grommets on the wires into the cutouts.
3   Reconnect the green/red striped wire to the neutral indicator switch.
4   Ensure that the two dowels are fitted correctly and smear Golden Hermatite or other jointing compound onto the crankcase joint face. Stick the gasket in position and fit the generator cover securing it with eight screws. Check the gearchange lever oil seal for any sign of deterioration or damage before fitting the cover.
5   Refit the sprocket cover and two screws if the engine is in the frame.
6   If the inspection cover has been removed, stick the gasket in position, again using Golden Hermatite, refit the cover and retain with the three screws. The condition of the 'O' rings on the three screws should be checked for any sign of deterioration or damage.

58 Refitting the engine/gearbox unit in the frame

1   Follow in reverse the procedure given in Section 5 of this Chapter with the following points borne in mind:
2   Check that the final drive chain link is fitted the correct way round. The closed end of the spring link should lead as the chain rotates.
3   Ensure that a new copper/asbestos joint ring is used in the exhaust port as a leakproof joint is essential for the correct running of the engine.
4   Ensure that the sealing washer of the drain plug is in good condition and fully tighten the drain plug. Refill the engine unit with oil of the recommended viscosity, to the correct level.

59 Starting and running the rebuilt engine

When the initial start-up is made, run the engine gently for the first few minutes in order to allow the oil to circulate throughout all parts of the engine. If the camshaft chain tensioner fitted is of a manual type, the tensioner should be adjusted in accordance with the instructions given in the Routine Maintenance Chapter. Remember that if a number of new parts have been fitted or if the engine has been rebored, it will be necessary to follow the original running-in instructions so that the new parts have ample opportunity to bed-down in a satisfactory manner. Check for oil leaks and/or blowing gaskets before the machine is run on the road.

58.3 Always use a new gasket for a leaktight joint

58.4 Refill the engine with the correct oil

60 Fault diagnosis: engine

Symptom	Cause	Remedy
Engine does not start	Lack of compression	
	Valve stuck open	Adjust tappet clearance.
	Worn valve guides	Renew.
	Valve timing incorrect	Check and adjust.
	Worn piston rings	Renew.
	Worn cylinder	Rebore.
	No spark at plug	
	Fouled or wet spark plug	Clean.
	Fouled contact breaker points	Clean.
	Incorrect ignition timing	Check and adjust.
	Open or short circuit in ignition	Check wiring and cut-out switch.

	No fuel flowing to carburettor	
	Blocked fuel tank cap vent hole	Clean.
	Blocked fuel tap	Clean.
	Faulty carburettor float valve	Renew.
	Blocked fuel pipe	Clean.
Engine stalls whilst running	Fouled spark plug or contact breaker points	Clean.
	Ignition timing incorrect	Adjust.
	Blocked fuel line or carburettor jets	Clean.
Noisy engine	Tappet noise:	
	Excessive tappet clearance	Check and reset.
	Weakened or broken valve spring	Renew springs.
	Knocking noise from cylinder:	
	Worn piston and cylinder noise	Rebore cylinder and fit oversize piston.
	Carbon in combustion chamber	Decoke engine.
	Worn gudgeon pin or connecting rod small end	Renew.
	Cam chain noise	Adjust.
	Stretched cam chain (rattle)	Renew chain.
	Worn cam sprocket or timing sprocket	Renew sprockets.
Engine noise	Excessive run-out of crankshaft	Renew.
	Worn crankshaft bearings (rumble)	Renew.
	Worn connecting rod or big end (knock)	Renew flywheel assembly.
	Worn transmission splines	Renew.
	Worn or binding transmission gear teeth	Renew gear pinions.
Smoking exhaust	Too much engine oil	Check oil level and adjust as necessary.
	Worn cylinder and piston rings	Rebore and fit oversize piston and rings.
	Worn valve guides	Renew.
	Damaged cylinder	Renew cylinder barrel and piston.
Insufficient power	Valve stuck open or incorrect tappets adjustment	Re-adjust.
	Weak valve springs	Renew.
	Valve timing incorrect	Check and reset.
	Worn cylinder and piston rings	Rebore and fit oversize piston and rings.
	Poor valve seatings	Grind in valves.
	Ignition timing incorrect	Check and adjust.
	Defective plug cap	Fit replacement.
	Dirty contact breaker points	Clean or renew.
Overheating	Accumulation of carbon on cylinder head	Decoke engine.
	Insufficient oil	Refill to specified level.
	Faulty oil pump and/or blocked oil passage	Strip and clean.
	Ignition timing too far retarded	Re-adjust.

61 Fault diagnosis: gearbox

Symptom	Cause	Remedy
Difficulty in engaging gears	Broken centre gear selector pawl or cam	Renew.
	Deformed gear selector	Repair or renew.
Machine jumps out of gear	Worn sliding gears on mainshaft and layshaft	Renew.
	Distorted or worn gear selector fork	Repair or renew.
	Weak gearchange drum stop spring	Renew spring
Gearchange lever fails to return normal position	Broken or displaced gearchange return spring	Renew or repair
Kickstart lever fails to return to normal position	Broken kickstart return spring	Renew spring.

Chapter 2 Clutch

Contents

Specifications

Clutch springs

Number	Four
Free length	19.6 mm (C50 model)
	21.4 mm (C70 model)
	27.0 mm (C90 model)
Minimum length	18.2 mm (C50 model)
	20.4 mm (C70 model)
	26.0 mm (C90 model)

Inserted clutch plates

Number	2 or 3, depending on model
Thickness	3.5 mm (C50 and C70 models)
	2.9 mm (C90 model)
Minimum thickness	3.1 mm (C50 and C70 models)
	2.4 mm (C90 model)

1 General description

The clutch is of the multi-plate type having two or three plain plates and two or three inserted plates depending on the model. The clutch is fully automatic in operation and interconnected with the gear change pedal so that it disengages and re-engages in the correct sequence.

2 Clutch assembly: dismantling

The clutch assembly complete is removed by following the procedure detailed in Chapter 1. Sections 12 and 13. When removed, the clutch can be broken down into its component parts as follows:
1 With the drive side (back) facing upwards, prise out the

2.1a Remove the large circlip ...

2.1b ... lift out the clutch centre ...

Fig. 2.1. Clutch assembly - C70 model

1	Clutch drum	10	Drive plate
2	Outer cover	11	Clutch spring (4 off)
3	Outer cover gasket	12	Clutch plate spring
4	Clutch centre		(4 off)
5	Bush	13	Clutch damping spring
6	Friction plate		(4 off)
7	Clutch plate	14	Clutch lever
8	Clutch plate	15	Cam plate
9	Clutch plate	16	Spring

17	Ball bearing retainer	26	Washer
18	Circlip	27	Washer (4 off)
19	Driver gear	28	Circlip
20	Clutch centre inner gear	29	Circlip
21	Primary drive gear	30	Roller (8 off)
22	Oil orifice	31	Screw (4 off)
23	Orifice spring	32	Screw (3 off)
24	Special nut	33	Ball bearing
25	Tab washer		

Fig. 2.2. Clutch assembly - C90 model

1	Clutch drum	11	Clutch spring (4 off)	19	Cam plate	29	Orifice spring
2	Outer cover	12	Clutch plate spring	20	Spring	30	Special nut
3	Outer cover gasket		(6 off)	21	Adjustable cam plate	31	Tab washer
4	Clutch centre	13	Clutch damping spring	22	Adjuster	32	Circlip
5	Bush		(4 off)	23	Ball bearing retainer	33	Washer (4 off)
6	Friction plate	14	Drive plate	24	Circlip	34	Screw (4 off)
7	Clutch plate	15	Bob-weight (24 off)	25	Spacer	35	Screw (2 off)
8	Clutch plate	16	Bob-weight clip	26	Drivegear	36	Circlip
9	Clutch plate	17	Bob-weight stop ring	27	Primary drive gear	37	Ball bearing
10	Clutch plate	18	Clutch lever	28	Oil orifice		

2.1c ... and remove the clutch plates

2.2 Remove the eight rollers which act as centrifugal weights

2.3 Remove the four screws to release the drive plate and springs

2.4 The circlip retains the clutch centre

3.4 Examine the clutch plates carefully

mm circlip from the rear of the clutch body and lift out the clutch centre assembly, complete with the clutch plates. The clutch plates will lift off the centre but care should be taken to avoid losing the four small plate separation springs that are located on the pins of the first clutch plate.

2   Remove the eight hardened steel rollers or on the C90 model the four shaped weights and clip.

3   Invert the clutch body and remove the four crosshead screws from the front face, unscrewing each a little at a time. This will release the drive plate, the four small damper springs and the four main clutch springs.

4   Removal of the retaining circlip from the clutch centre will permit the clutch drive gear to be separated.

3   Clutch: examination and renovation

1   Check the condition of the clutch drive to ensure none of the teeth are chipped, broken or badly worn.

2   Give the plain and the inserted clutch plates a wash with a paraffin/petrol mix and check that they are not buckled or distorted. Remove all traces of clutch insert debris, otherwise a gradual build-up will affect clutch action.

3   Visual inspection will show whether the tongues of the clutch plates have become burred and whether indentations have formed in the slots with which they engage. Burrs should be removed with a file, which can also be used to dress the slots, provided the depth of the indentations is not great.

4   Check the thickness of the friction linings in the inserted plates, referring to the Specifications section of this Chapter for the serviceable limits. If the linings have worn to, or below these limits, the plates should be renewed. Worn linings promote clutch slip.

5   Check also the free length of the clutch springs. The recommended serviceable limits are also in the Specification section. Do not attempt to stretch the springs if they have compressed. They must be renewed when they reach the serviceable limit, as a complete set.

6   Check the condition of the roller thrust bearing in the clutch outer plate.

4   Clutch operating mechanism: examination and renovation

The automatic clutch fitted to these models is designed so that as the engine speed increases, eight hardened steel rollers increase their pressure on the clutch plates through being thrown outwards along their respective tapered tracks by centrifugal force. Four small diameter compression springs assist the clutch plates to free, and four large diameter compression springs supply additional pressure when the rollers reach the end of their tracks.

A quick acting three-start thread mechanism is incorporated in an extension of the drive gear to apply pressure when the kickstart is operated, or when the machine is on the over-run.

The clutch is completely disengaged each time the gear operating pedal is moved, through a direct linkage between the gear change lever spindle and the clutch withdrawal mechanism.

1   Check the condition of the roller ramps in the clutch drive plate and the roller contact area. Excessive wear in these areas is often the cause of engine stalling, fierce clutch engagement and difficulty in gear changing. Replace the worn parts.

2   It is rarely necessary to replace the eight rollers or the clutch housing, unless the rollers show evidence of wear and the clutch housing has roller indentations. This type of wear is caused by poor gear changing, usually by releasing the gear pedal too fast when moving away from a standstill or changing gear.

3   The C90 model uses a different mode of operation involving the use of four weights. The earliest problem of wear is therefore obviated even though the clutch operates on the centrifugal principle.

5   Clutch: reassembly

1   Reassemble the clutch components by following the dismantling procedure in reverse.

2   The built-up clutch is then replaced on the splined end of the crankshaft, following the engine reassembly procedure given in Chapter 1, Section 50. A torque setting of 27.5 - 32.5 lbs ft is recommended for the sleeve nut that retains the clutch in position. Make sure the tab washer is bent over, to lock the sleeve nut in position.

3   Replace the oil filters and cover reassembly as described in Chapter 1, Section 51, ensuring that the clutch is adjusted according to the details given in the next section of this Chapter.

6   Clutch: adjustment

1   Clutch adjustment is provided by means of an adjustable screw and locknut located in the centre of the clutch cover. Slacken off the 10 mm locknut and turn the adjusting screw firstly in the clockwise direction, to ensure there is no end pressure on the clutch pushrod.

2   Turn the adjusting screw anti-clockwise until pressure can be felt on the end. Turn back (clockwise) for approximately 1/8th of a turn, and tighten the locknut, making sure the screw does not turn. Clutch adjustment should now be correct.

7   Clutch: correct operation

1   As the special starting mechanism operates when starting the engine, clutch slip can only be detected when the machine is being ridden, by the fact that the engine speed will increase with no increase in road speed.

2   Clutch drag is characterised by the engine having a tendency to stall or the machine starting to move forward, when first gear is engaged, with the engine running at tickover speed.

3   Refer to the fault diagnosis chart, Section 8, for possible causes for the above symptom.

4   Note that a fast tickover speed will cause the machine to snatch when first gear is engaged during the pullaway from a standstill.

3.6 Check the condition of the ball bearing

6.1 Clutch is adjusted with the cover attached

8   Fault diagnosis: clutch

Symptom	Cause	Remedy
Clutch slips	Incorrect adjustment	Re-adjust.
	Weak clutch springs	Renew set of four.
	Worn or distorted pressure plate	Renew.
	Distorted clutch plates	Renew.
	Worn friction plates	Renew.
Knocking noise from clutch	Loose clutch centre	Renew clutch.
Clutch does not fully disengage	Incorrect adjustment	Re-adjust
	Uneven clutch spring tension	Re-adjust.
	Distorted clutch plates	Renew.

Chapter 3 Fuel system and lubrication

Contents

Specifications

Petrol tank

			C50	C70	C90
Capacity	... ...		3.0 litres (5.3 Imp pints)	4.5 litres (7.9 Imp pints)	5.5 litres (9.7 Imp pints)

Carburettor

		C50	C70	C90
Make	... ...	Keihin Seiki		
Type	... ...	DP13N13 (1000 - 110)	DP13N14AI (1000 - 112)	PW15HAI (1000 - 109)
Main jet	... ...	70	75	75
Slow running jet	... ...	35	35	40
Throttle slide	... ...	2.0	2.5	2.0
Needle	... ...	13239 - 3 stage	13243 - 3 stage	16332 - 2 stage
Slow running screw	... ...	1 - 1 1/4 turns out	1 3/8 - 1 5/8 turns out	3/8 - 1 1/8 turns out
Needle jet bore	... ...	3.0 mm	2.10 mm	2.60 mm

Oil pump

Outer rotor to pump body clearance	0.1 - 0.15 mm (0.004 - 0.006 inch)
Inner and outer rotor end clearance	0.02 - 0.07 mm (0.0008 - 0.0028 inch)
Rotor tip clearance	0.15 mm (0.006 inch)
replace if over	0.2 mm (0.008 inch)

1 General description

The fuel system comprises a fuel tank from which petrol is fed by gravity to the float chamber of the carburettor. The open frame layout necessitates the use of a specially-shaped petrol tank that is located immediately below the nose of the dualseat. On these models, the petrol tap is incorporated in the top of the carburettor float chamber.

All machines are fitted with a carburettor of Keihin manufacture, the model depending on the type of machine to which the carburettor is fitted. All carburettors have a manually-operated choke and employ a throttle slide and needle arrangement for controlling the petrol/air mixture administered to the engine.

2 Legshield: removal

1 The plastic legshield assembly encloses the engine unit, to enhance the clean appearance of the machine. There are suitable holes and blanking discs to enable the simplest of the adjusting tasks to be carried out without necessitating removal of the legshields, but whenever access is required for more complex tasks, the legshield assembly must be removed.

2 Place the machine on the centre stand and make sure it is standing firmly, on level ground.

3 Remove the side panels to obtain the toolkit and reveal the battery. Unscrew the fuse holder and remove the fuse, to isolate the battery, eliminating all risks of electrical mishap.

4 Remove the domed nut and the air cleaner lid.

3.5a Remove the four fixing bolts ...

3.5b ... and release the petrol pipes

5.3 The dismantled petrol tap

5   Slacken the nuts holding the rear of the legshield and remove the clamping band, if fitted. Remove the four bolts holding the legshield and pull their spacers clear. The legshield assembly will now lift clear.

3   Petrol tank: removal and replacement

1   It is unlikely that there will be need to remove the petrol tank completely unless the machine has been laid up and rust has formed inside or it needs reconditioning. The engine/gear unit can be removed from the frame without having to detach the tank. The ignition coil is mounted inside the frame and the tank has to be removed first, to gain access.
2   As the petrol tap is an integral part of the carburettor, the petrol tank must be drained before it is removed.
3   Release the clips, pull both of the petrol feed pipes off the carburettor and let them drain into a suitable container.
4   Lift the dualseat and either remove it as described in Chapter 5 or fix it securely to avoid its falling forward at a crucial stage.
5   Remove the four bolts and washers holding the tank to the frame. Gently lift the tank, release the clips and pull off both of the petrol pipes. The tank will now lift clear. Leave the pipes threaded into the frame, to ease assembly.
6   To replace the tank, reverse the procedure described in the preceding paragraphs, ensuring that the petrol pipe with the red stripe is connected to the reserve pipes on the tank and carburettor.

4   Petrol feed pipes: examination and renewal

1   The petrol feed pipes are made of synthetic rubber and a check that they are not cracked or chafed, where they pass through the frame, should be made, as leaking petrol can cause a fire. Ensure that the wire retaining clips on each end are present, in good condition and properly located.
2   To renew the petrol feed pipes it is necessary to remove the petrol tank, as described in Section 3, and the battery as described in Chapter 7, to permit access to the clips and the inside of the frame. Ensure that the petrol pipe with the red stripe is connected to the reserve pipes on the tank and carburettor.

5   Petrol tap: removal and replacement

1   The petrol tap is a three position open - reserve - closed type, built as an integral part of the carburettor.
2   It can be dismantled without removing the carburettor but the petrol tank will have to be drained as described in Section 3.
3   Remove the two screws, the tap cover, the wave washer, the lever plate and the rubber sealing disc. Check for deterioration of the rubber disc and reassemble in the reverse order.
4   Refit the petrol pipes and refill the tank.

6   Carburettor: general description

Various types of Keihin carburettor are fitted to the Honda 50 cc - 90 cc models, the exact specifications depending on the designation of the model. Air is drawn into all the carburettors, via an air filter with a removable element. The conventional throttle slide and needle arrangement works in conjunction with the main jet, to control the amount of petrol/air mixture administered to the engine. There is also a slow running jet with an adjustable air screw, to control idling at low speeds, and a manually-operated choke, to aid cold starting.

Fig. 3.1. Carburettor assembly - C70 model

1	Complete carburettor gasket set	5	Slide top assembly	9	Carburettor assembly	15	Spring washer (3 off)
2	Float and needle assembly	6	Float chamber top assembly	10	Carburettor assembly	16	Overflow tube
3	Needle and jet set	7	Slow running and throttle stop screws	11	Cable sleeve	17	Breather tube
4	Needle and jet set			12	Screw (2 off)	18	Tube clip (2 off)
		8	Slide and return spring	13	Screw (2 off)	19	Main jet
				14	Screw	20	Slow running jet

7 Carburettor: removal

Engine removed from the frame

1 If the engine has already been removed from the frame and, on the C90 model, the inlet tube removed, the carburettor will be attached to the control cable, the petrol pipes and to the synthetic rubber intake tube. Release the clip and pull the carburettor out of the rubber tube after the petrol tank has been drained as described in Section 3.

Engine still in the frame

2 If the engine is still in the frame the carburettor is sandwiched between the top of the engine and the main frame tube.

3 Drain the petrol tank as described in Section 3.

4 Disconnect the wires to the horn at the snap connectors. Release the spring clips at both ends of the rubber intake tube and pull the tube clear.

5 Remove the two nuts and washers and pull the carburettor off the engine or the inlet tube.

6 Make sure the 'O' ring in the carburettor flange is not lost.

8 Carburettor: dismantling (C50 and C70 models)

1 At this stage, the carburettor is still attached to the control cable and to remove it completely the carburettor top has to be unscrewed and the slide and needle pulled out.

2 Compress the slide return spring and unhook the throttle cable. The slide, the needle with its spring clip, the w-shaped spring, the return spring and the carburettor top will then slide off the cable.

3 Remove the three screws holding the float chamber top in position and pull the top clear. Remove the float needle seat from the underside of the float chamber top. Lift the filter chamber, the sealing ring, and the petrol filter out of the float chamber top.

4 Lift the float and needle assembly out of the float chamber.

5 Remove the throttle stop screw and the slow running air screw from the side of the carburettor, taking care not to lose the small springs.

6 Remove the blanking plug, with its 'O' ring, and push out from the throttle slide chamber the needle jet. Remove the adjacent slow running jet.

8.2 The dismantled slide assembly

8.3a Remove the screws and the float chamber top ...

8.3b ... and unscrew the float valve seat ...

8.3c ... and remove the petrol filter

8.4 The float assembly will lift out

8.5a Remove the throttle stop screw ...

8.5b ... and the slow running mixture screw

8.6a Remove the sealing plug ...

8.6b ... and the needle jet from one hole ...

Fig. 3.2. Carburettor assembly - C90 model

1   *Complete carburettor gasket set*
2   *Float needle valve set*
3   *Needle and jet set*
4   *Float assembly*
5   *Slide top assembly*
6   *Float chamber assembly*
7   *Slow running and throttle stop screws*
8   *Slide and return spring*
9   *Carburettor assembly*
10   *Needle jet holder*
11   *Cable sleeve*
12   *Bolt*
13   *Screw (2 off)*
14   *Screw (2 off)*
15   *Screw (2 off)*
16   *Washer (2 off)*
17   *Breather tube*
18   *Overflow tube*
19   *Tube clip (2 off)*
20   *Main jet*
21   *Slow running jet*

7   Remove the two blanking plugs that are close to the mounting flange and remove the main jet, using a small screwdriver,
from the carburettor body.
8   Remove the float chamber drain screw.
9   The choke flap is rivetted into position and cannot easily
be removed.

9 Carburettor: dismantling (C90 model only)

1   At this stage, the carburettor is still attached to the control
cable and to remove it completely, the carburettor top has to be
unscrewed and the slide and needle pulled out.
2   Compress the slide return spring and unhook throttle cable.
The slide, the needle with its spring clip, the w-shaped spring,
the return spring and the carburettor top will then slide off the
cable.
3   Remove the two screws holding the float chamber in position
and pull the chamber clear. Remove the two screws on the
end of the float chamber to release the blanking plate, sealing
ring and petrol filter. Remove the float chamber drain screw.
4   Invert the carburettor body and push out the float pivot pin.
This releases the float and the float needle. Carefully remove the
float needle from the float.
5   Remove from the underside of the carburettor body the
float needle seat, the slow running jet and from the centre the
main jet, the jet holder and the needle jet.
6   Remove the throttle stop screw and the slow running air
screw from the side of the carburettor, taking care not to loose
the small springs.
7   The choke flap is rivetted into position and cannot easily be
removed.

10 Carburettor: cleaning, examining and reassembling

1   Thoroughly clean all the parts paying particular attention to
the internal passageways of the carburettor body, the bottom of
the float chamber and any other places where sediment may
collect.
2   Check that none of the springs are weak or broken.
3   Check for wear on the slide and carburettor body as air leaks
round the slide can cause weak mixture problems.
4   Check for ridges on the conical sealing portion of the float
needle.
5   Check the condition of the float and shake it to see if there is

8.6c ... and the slow running jet from the one adjacent

8.7a Remove the two sealing plugs ...

8.7b ... and the main jet

8.8 Remove the float chamber drain screw

10.5 Check the float assembly for damage

12.1 Clean the air filter carefully as it is only paper

any petrol inside. The float is non-repairable and should be renewed if damaged or punctured.

6　Check that all gaskets, sealing washers or rubber seals are in good condition. Preferably renew them when reassembling as leaking petrol can cause a fire.

7　When reassembling the carburettor, follow the dismantling instructions in reverse, ensuring that the needle clip is in its correct groove.

8　The various sizes of the jets, throttle slide and needle are predetermined by the manufacturer and should not require modification. Check with the Specifications list if there is any doubt about the values fitted.

11 Carburettor: adjustments

1　All adjustments should be made when the engine is at normal working temperature.

2　To adjust the slow running speed the throttle cable should be slackened to ensure that it is the throttle stop screw that is holding the slide and not the cable. Set the throttle stop screw so that the engine runs at a fast tick-over speed.

3　Screw in or out the air screw until the engine runs evenly, without hunting or misfiring. Reduce the engine speed by unscrewing the throttle stop and re-adjust the air screw, if necessary. Do not arrive at a setting where the engine ticks over too slowly, otherwise there is risk that it may stall when the throttle is closed, during normal running.

4　As a rough guide, the air screw should be positioned from one to one and a quarter complete turns out from the fully closed position.

5　The amount of throttle slide cutaway, size of main jet, size of needle jet and size of slow running jet are pre-determined by the manufacturer and should be correct for the model in which they are used. Check with the Specifications, page 67. The throttle needle position can be varied, by removing and replacing the needle clip. Under normal circumstances, the needle should be positioned in the second or third notch, measured from the top.

6　The slow running jet controls engine speed up to approximately 1/8th throttle and the degree of throttle slide cutaway from 1/8th to ¼ throttle. Thereafter the needle jet takes over, up to ¾ throttle, and main jet size controls the final ¾ to full throttle. These stages are only approximate; there is a certain amount of overlap.

7　Readjust the throttle cable to remove any excess play but leave a small amount of slack to avoid the engine speed increasing when the handlebars are turned.

13.2a Remove the swinging arm nut to release the silencer ...

13.2b ... and the collets to release the exhaust pipe

12 Air filter: location and cleaning

1 The air filter is located on top of the main frame tube, immediately behind the steering head. It is clearly visible when the the legshield assembly has been removed.

2 To clean the air filter, remove the detachable element and tap it lightly to remove accumulated dust. Blow from the inside de with compressed air, or brush the exterior with a light brush. Remember the element is made from paper. If it is torn or damaged, fit a replacement.

3 Oil or water will reduce the efficiency of the filter element and may upset the carburation. Renew any suspect element.

4 It is advisable to replace the element at less than the recommended 6,000 miles if the machine is used in very dusty conditions. The usual signs of a filter element in need of replacement are reduced performance, misfiring and a tendency for the carburation to run rich.

5 On no account should the machine be run without the filter element in place because this will have an adverse effect on carburation.

13 Exhaust system: cleaning

1 Although the exhaust system on a four-stroke does not require such frequent attention as that of the two-stroke, it is nevertheless advisable to inspect the complete system from time to time in order to ensure a build-up of carbon does not cause back pressure. If an engine is nearing the stage where a rebore is necessary, it is advisable to check the exhaust system more frequently. The oily nature of the exhaust gases will cause a more rapid build-up of sludge.

2 The complete exhaust system is removed from the machine by detaching the swinging arm nut, the two nuts and flange at the exhaust port, and pulling the exhaust clear. The two half collets will fall clear from the exhaust pipe but the exhaust gasket will need to be prised out of the cylinder head and consequently will need renewing. If this joint is not an airtight seal, the engine will tend to backfire on the over-run.

3 A 10 mm bolt in the extreme end of the silencer retains the detachable baffle assembly in position. If this bolt is withdrawn, the baffle tube can be pulled clear of the silencer body, for cleaning.

4 Tap the baffle to remove loose carbon and work with a wire brush, if necessary. If there is a heavy build-up of carbon or oily sludge, it may be necessary to use a blow lamp to burn out these deposits.

5 The exhaust pipe and silencer are one unit and if a large amount of carbon has built up inside it is necessary to fill the

silencer with a solution of caustic soda after blocking up one end. If possible, leave the caustic soda solution within the silencer overnight, before draining off and washing out thoroughly with water.

6 Caustic soda is highly corrosive and every care should be taken when mixing and handling the solution. Keep the solution away from the skin and more particularly the eyes. The wearing of rubber gloves is advised whilst the solution is being mixed and used.

7 The solution is prepared by adding 3 lbs of caustic soda to 1 gallon of COLD water, whilst stirring. Add the caustic soda a little at a time and NEVER add the water to the chemical. The solution will become hot during the mixing process, which is why cold water must be used.

8 Make sure the used caustic soda solution is disposed of safely, preferably by diluting with a large amount of water. Do not allow the solution to come into contact with aluminium castings because it will react violently with this metal.

9 To reassemble the exhaust system reverse the dismantling procedure, ensuring that the baffle assembly retaining bolt is fully tightened.

10 Do not run the machine without the baffle tube in position. Although the changed engine note may give the illusion of greater speed, the net effect will be a marked drop in performance as a result of changes in carburation. There is also risk of prosecution as a result of the excessive noise.

14 Lubrication system

1 Oil is picked up from the oil compartment in the crankcase by the oil pump, via an oil filter screen which filters out any impurities that may otherwise damage the pump itself. The pump delivers oil, under pressure, to the right-hand crankcase where it follows the routes listed below:

a) *The oil passes through a drilling in the clutch cover, through the pressure release orifice in the centre of the clutch, through the centrifugal oil filter, and into the crankshaft, to lubricate the big end and main bearings.*

b) *The oil passes up the side of one of the holding down studs, through the cylinder barrel and into the cylinder head, where a side cover distributes the oil to the rocker pins and the camshaft. Some of the oil lubricates the camchain on its return, although the C50 and C70 models have an oil return passageway.*

c) *On the C90 model only, there are additional drillings within the crankcases to feed oil to the mainshaft and layshaft plain bearings.*

13.3 The baffle tube is removable for cleaning

15.3 The gauze oil filter fits in a slot in the crankcase

Fig. 3.3. Clutch cover and oil pump - C70 model

1	Clutch cover	8	Inner rotor	15	Clip	21	Bolt
2	Clutch cover gasket	9	Outer rotor	16	Washer	22	Screw (3 off)
3	Oil pump gasket	10	Driveshaft	17	Oil seal	23	Screw (6 off)
4	Oil pump assembly	11	Dowel	18	O-ring	24	Screw (2 off)
5	Oil pump body	12	Dipstick	19	O-ring	25	Nut
6	Oil pump cover	13	Adjustable camplate	20	Bolt (2 off)	26	Washer (3 off)
7	Cover gasket	14	Adjuster				

2   The remainder of the engine components are lubricated by splash from the oil content of the sump.

15 Oil filters and pressure relief valve: location and cleaning

1   As explained in the previous Section, there are two filters in the lubrication system, a square section gauze filter screen that slots into a cavity in the right-hand crankcase, and a filter of the centrifugal type that is attached to the outer face of the clutch.
2   Both can be removed for cleaning when the procedure given in Chapter 1 Section 12 is followed.
3   The gauze filter should be cleaned by immersing it in petrol and if necessary, brushing it with a soft haired brush to remove any impurities or foreign matter. Allow it to dry before replacement. If for any reason the gauze is damaged, the complete filter must be renewed.
4   The centrifugal filter should be washed out with petrol and any impurities or foreign matter removed in similar fashion. Dry the assembly with clean rag, prior to reassembly. Before replacing the end cover and tightening the screws, check the condition of the sealing gasket.
5   When using petrol for washing purposes, take extreme care as petrol vapour is highly inflammable. Cleaning should preferably be accomplished in the open air or in well-ventilated surroundings away from any naked flames.
6   In the centre of the clutch release mechanism there is a spring loaded orifice that acts as a pressure relief valve. Ensure that the hole in the orifice is clear, that the spring is in good condition and that the orifice is free to move within the release mechanism.
7   For the reassembly sequence, refer to Chapter 1 Section 51.

16 Trochoidal oil pump: description and location

1   The trochoid oil pump is located behind the clutch, where it is retained to the right-hand crankcase by three bolts. It is extremely unlikely that the pump will require attention under normal circumstances and should not be dismantled unnecessarily.
2   The pump comprises an inner and an outer rotor. The pumping action is provided by the differences in the shape and number of teeth between the inner and the outer rotors.

15.4 The clutch outer plate forms the centrifugal oil filter

15.6 Check the pressure relief valve

17.2 Remove the cover to check oil pump operation

17.5 Remove the pump to renew any worn parts

17 Trochoidal oil pump: removal, renovation and replacement

1   If the pump is suspected in the event of a lubrication
failure, it can be dismantled after it has been detached from the
engine unit by referring to Sections 12, 13 and 23 of Chapter 1.
2   Remove the three screws and the rotor cover plate to gain
access to the inner and outer rotors.
3   Clearances between the various internal components

can be checked with the wear limits given in the Specifications
Section of this Chapter.
4   To reassemble the oil pump, fit the outer rotor, the inner
rotor and feed the drive shaft into position rotating the rotors
if necessary to fully engage the shaft. Stick the cover gasket in
position, using a film of grease, and refit the cover and screws.
5   Refit the oil pump as described in Chapter 1 Section 40 and
complete the engine reassembly as described in Chapter 1
Sections 50 and 51.

18 Fault diagnosis: fuel system and lubrication

Symptom	Cause	Remedy
Excessive fuel consumption	Air cleaner choked or restricted	Clean or renew.
	Fuel leaking from carburettor. Float sticking	Check all unions and gaskets. Float needle seat needs cleaning.
	Badly worn or distorted carburettor	Renew.
	Jet needle setting too high	Adjust to figure given in Specifications.
	Main jet too large or loose	Fit correct jet or tighten if necessary.
	Carburettor flooding	Check float valve and renew if worn.
Idling speed too high	Throttle stop screw in too far.	Adjust screw.
	Carburettor top loose	Tighten top.
	Pilot jet incorrectly adjusted	Refer to relevant paragraph in this Chapter.
	Throttle cable sticking	Disconnect and lubricate or replace.
Engine dies after running a short while	Blocked air hole in filler cap	Clean.
	Dirt or water in carburettor	Remove and clean out.
General lack of performance	Weak mixture; float needle stuck in seat	Remove float chamber or float and clean.
	Air leak at carburettor joint	Check joint to eliminate leakage, and fit new O-ring.
Engine does not respond to throttle	Throttle cable sticking	See above.
	Petrol octane rating too low	Use higher grade (star rating) petrol.
Engine runs hot and is noisy	Lubrication failure	Stop engine immediately and investigate cause. Slacken cylinder head nut to check oil circulation. Do not restart until cause is found and rectified.

Chapter 4 Ignition system

Contents

Specifications

	C50	C70	C90
Generator			
Make	Hitachi Seisakusho	Mitsubishi Denki or Nippon Denso	Kokusan Denki
Type	F120	FAZ or 37000-026-0	EG26
Coil			
Make	Hitachi Seisakusho	Hitachi Seisakusho	Kokusan Denki
Type	CM61 - 08	CM61 - 08	ST 78
Spark plug			
Make	NGK or Champion	NGK or Champion	NGK or Champion
Type	C - 7HS Z - 8 or Z - 10	C - 7HS Z - 8 or Z - 10	D - 6HS or P7
Gap	0.6 - 0.7 mm (0.024 - 0.028 inch)	0.6 - 0.7 mm (0.024 - 0.028 inch)	0.6 - 0.7 mm (0.024 - 0.028 inch)
Contact breaker gap ...	0.3 - 0.4 mm (0.012 - 0.016 inch)	0.3 - 0.4 mm (0.012 - 0.016 inch)	0.3 - 0.4 mm (0.012 - 0.016 inch)

1 General description

The system used for producing the spark which is necessary to ignite the petrol/air mixture in the combustion chamber differs slightly between that used for the C50 and C70 models and the C90 model.

In the C50 and C70 system, the flywheel generator produces the electrical power which is fed directly to the ignition coil, mounted inside the frame. The condenser and contact breaker assembly are mounted inside the flywheel generator, where, with the help of an automatic advance and retard mechanism, they determine the exact moment at which the spark will occur. The ignition switch shorts out the ignition system when it is switched off.

In the C90 system, the battery produces the electrical power, which is fed through a fuse and the ignition switch to the ignition coil, mounted inside the frame. The condenser is mounted on the end of the ignition coil. The contact breaker assembly and automatic advance and retard mechanism are mounted on the end of the camshaft, on the left-hand side of the cylinder head. The generator will produce sufficient power for starting the engine if the battery is flat.

When the contact breaker points separate, the electrical circuit is interrupted and a high tension voltage is developed across the points of the spark plug, which jumps the air gap and ignites the mixture.

2 Legshield: removal

1 The plastic legshield assembly encloses the engine unit to enhance the clean appearance of the machine. There are suitable holes and blanking discs to enable the simplest of the adjusting tasks to be carried out without removing the legshield, but whenever access is required for more complex tasks the legshield assembly must be removed.
2 Place the machine on the centre stand and make sure it is standing firmly on level ground.
3 Remove the side panels to obtain the toolkit and reveal the battery. Unscrew the fuse holder and remove the fuse to isolate the battery, eliminating all risks of electrical mishap.
4 Remove the domed nut and the air cleaner lid.
5 Slacken the nuts holding the rear of the legshield assembly and remove the clamping band if fitted. Remove the four bolts holding the legshields and pull their spacers clear. The legshields will now lift clear.

Fig. 4.1. Flywheel generator and cover - C70 model

1	Generator cover	16	Grommet
2	Contact breaker assembly	17	Screw
3	Felt wick	18	Screw
4	Condenser	19	Washer
5	Inspection cover	20	Oil seal
6	Cover gasket	21	Oil seal
7	Ignition coil	22	O-ring
8	Generator assembly	23	O-ring (2 off)
9	Generator assembly	24	Screw (2 off)
10	Rotor	25	Screw
11	Stator plate assembly	26	Screw (2 off)
12	Stator plate assembly	27	Screw (2 off)
13	Lighting coil	28	Nut
14	Lighting coil	29	Washer
15	Grommet	30	Washer (2 off)

Fig. 4.2. Alternator and covers - C90 model

1	Alternator cover	6	Gearchange lever	11	Washer	16 Screw (3 off)
2	Sprocket cover	7	Alternator assembly	12	Screw (3 off)	17 Screw (9 off)
3	Alternator cover gasket	8	Rotor	13	Oil seal	18 Screw
4	Inspection cover	9	Stator assembly	14	O-ring (3 off)	19 Dowel
5	Cover gasket	10	Bolt	15	Bolt	

3 Flywheel generators: checking outputs

The output from either of the two types of generator used can be checked only with specialised test equipment of the multi-meter type. It is unlikely that the average owner/rider will have access to this equipment or instruction in its use. In consequence, if the performance of a generator is suspect, it should be checked by a Honda agent or an auto-electrical expert.

4 Ignition coil: checking, removal and replacement

1 The ignition coil is a sealed unit, designed to give long service. If a weak spark and difficult starting cause its performance to be suspect, it should be tested by a Honda agent or an auto-electrical expert. A faulty coil must be renewed. It is not practicable to effect a repair.
2 To gain access to the coil, the petrol tank must first be removed as described in Chapter 3, Section 3. The battery and its holder will also have to be removed, as described in Chapter 7, Section 3 to gain access to the inside of the frame where the coil is mounted and retained by two nuts. Remove the nuts and carefully pull the coil part way out so that the wires can be disconnected at the snap connectors. Pull the plug cap off the plug, unscrew it from the plug lead and feed the plug lead through the clip and back into the frame above the engine, to allow the ignition coil to pull clear.
3 Reassembly is the reverse of the removal procedure.

5 Contact breaker: adjustment

1 The C50 and C70 models use an ignition system commonly referred to as an 'energy transfer' system. The subtle advantage of this system is that the contact breaker adjustment is used to adjust the ignition timing. The resulting maximum contact breaker gap should be between 0.3 mm and 0.4 mm (0.012 in and 0.016 in). If it is outside these limits, the contact breaker assembly should be renewed, since it is worn out. The ignition timing section describes the method of adjustment. If it should be necessary to remove the contact breaker assembly for further attention, or renewal, it will be necessary to withdraw the flywheel generator from the crankshaft, following the procedure described in Chapter 1, Section 7.
2 The C90 model uses a conventional ignition system in which the contact breaker gap is adjusted first and the backplate adjusted to obtain the correct ignition timing.

3 Remove the two screws and the contact breaker cover on the left-hand side of the cylinder head.
4 Rotate the engine until the contact breaker is in its fully open position. Examine the faces of the contacts. If they are pitted or burnt it will be necessary to remove them for further attention, as described in Section 6 of this Chapter.
5 Check the contact breaker gap to see if it is between 0.3 mm and 0.4 mm (0.012 and 0.016 in). To adjust the contact breaker gap, slacken the two screws that hold the contact breaker assembly and using a small screwdriver in the slot provided, ease the assembly to the correct position. Tighten the screws and recheck the gap to ensure that the assembly has not moved.
6 It is always advisable to check the ignition timing, especially if the contact breaker gap has been reset. It will almost certainly require readjustment in this latter case.
7 Ensure that the sealing gasket is either renewed or is in good condition, before refitting the contact breaker cover and screws.

6 Contact breaker assembly: removal, renovation and replacement

1 If the contact breaker points are burned, pitted or badly worn, they should be removed for dressing. If it is necessary to remove a substantial amount of material before the faces can be restored, the points should be renewed.
2 To remove the contact breaker assembly, access must be gained as described in the preceding Section. Slacken and remove the nut at the end of the moving contact return spring. Remove the spring and plain washer and detach the spring. Note that an insulating washer is located beneath the spring, to prevent the electrical current from being earthed.
3 Remove the spring clip from the moving contact pivot and the insulating washer. Withdraw the moving contact, which is integral with the fibre rocker arm.
4 Remove the screws that retain the fixed contact plate and withdraw the plate complete with contact.
5 The points should be dressed with an oilstone or fine emery cloth. Keep them absolutely square during the dressing operation, otherwise they will make angular contact when they are replaced and will quickly burn away.
6 Replace the contacts by reversing the dismantling procedure. Take particular care to replace the insulating washers in the correct sequence, otherwise the points will be isolated electrically and the ignition system will not function.

4.2 The ignition coil is mounted inside the frame

6.3 Remove the screw and release the wire to withdraw the contact breaker assembly

Fig. 4.3. Contact breaker assembly - C90 model

1 Contact breaker base	6 Automatic advance retard	11 Base gasket	17 Oil seal
2 Contact breaker assembly	assembly	12 Coil assembly	18 Washer
3 Backplate	7 Condenser	13 Suppressor cap	19 Bolt
4 Contact breaker assembly	8 Base assembly	14 Clip	20 Screw (2 off)
5 Felt wick	9 Cover	15 Washer (3 off)	21 Screw (3 off)
	10 Cover gasket	16 Washer (2 off)	22 Screw (2 off)

7.5 The condenser is mounted on the stator plate

8.2 When the 'F' mark lines up with the crankcase mark the points should be about to open

9.1 Check the action of the automatic advance/retard mechanism

7   Condenser: removal and replacement

1   A condenser is included in the contact breaker circuitry to prevent arcing across the contact breaker points as they separate. It is connected in parallel with the points and if a fault develops, ignition failure will occur.

2   If the engine is difficult to start or if misfiring occurs, it is possible that the condenser has failed. To check, separate the contact breaker points by hand whilst the ignition is switched on. If a spark occurs across the points and they have a blackened or burnt appearance, the condenser can be regarded as unserviceable.

3   It is not possible to check the condenser without the necessary test equipment. It is best to fit a replacement condenser and observe the effect on engine performance, especially in view of its low cost.

4   To remove the condenser on the C90 model, follow the procedure described in Section 4, for removing the ignition coil, as the condenser is clamped to the end of this coil. Slacken the clamp and pull the condenser clear.

5   To remove the condenser on the C50 and C70 models, follow the procedure described in Chapter 1, Section 7, for removing the flywheel generator, as the condenser is mounted on the stator plate. Unsolder the wires on the condenser, remove the fixing screw and pull the condenser clear.

6   Reassemble by reversing the dismantling procedure. Take care not to overheat the condenser when resoldering the wires into position as the insulation is very easily damaged by heat.

8   Ignition timing: checking and re-setting

1   To check the ignition timing, remove the generator inspection cover or, in the case of the C90 model, the contact breaker cover on the left-hand side of the cylinder head.

2   If the ignition timing is correct, the contact breaker points will be about to separate when the 'F' line scribed on the rotor of the flywheel coincides exactly with an arrow or an indentation or similar scribe mark on the left-hand crankcase or cover.

3   On the C50 and C70 models having the 'energy transfer' system, the ignition timing is varied by adjusting the contact breaker gap. Slacken the screw holding the contact breaker assembly, and using a small screwdriver in the slot provided, ease the assembly to the correct position. Tighten the screw and recheck the ignition timing. Check that the contact breaker gap is between 0.3 mm and 0.4 mm (0.012 in and 0.016 in), renewing the assembly, if outside these limits.

4   On the C90 models, which have a more conventional system, the ignition timing is adjusted by moving the contact breaker backplate. Before checking the ignition timing, always make sure the contact breaker gap is correct first. The backplate holding the complete contact breaker assembly is slotted, to permit a limited range of adjustment. If the two crosshead screws are slackened a little, the plate can be turned until the points commence to separate, and then locked in this position by tightening the screws.

5   After checking the timing, rotate the engine and check again before replacing the covers. The accuracy of the ignition timing is critical in terms of both engine performance and petrol consumption. Even a small error in setting will have a noticeable effect.

9   Automatic advance unit: location and checking action

1   Fixed ignition timing is of little advantage as the engine speed increases and provision is made to advance the timing by centrifugal means, using a balance weight assembly located behind the contact breaker assembly or within the rotor of the flywheel magneto generator. A check is not needed unless the action of the unit is in doubt.

2   To check the action of the unit it is first necessary to withdraw the contact breaker assembly complete from the C90

Electrode gap check - use a wire type gauge for best results

Electrode gap adjustment - bend the side electrode using the correct tool

Normal condition - A brown, tan or grey firing end indicates that the engine is in good condition and that the plug type is correct

Ash deposits - Light brown deposits encrusted on the electrodes and insulator, leading to misfire and hesitation. Caused by excessive amounts of oil in the combustion chamber or poor quality fuel/oil

Carbon fouling - Dry, black sooty deposits leading to misfire and weak spark. Caused by an over-rich fuel/air mixture, faulty choke operation or blocked air filter

Oil fouling - Wet oily deposits leading to misfire and weak spark. Caused by oil leakage past piston rings or valve guides (4-stroke engine), or excess lubricant (2-stroke engine)

Overheating - A blistered white insulator and glazed electrodes. Caused by ignition system fault, incorrect fuel, or cooling system fault

Worn plug - Worn electrodes will cause poor starting in damp or cold weather and will also waste fuel

model or withdraw the rotor of the flywheel magneto generator. Refer to Chapter 1.7 for the dismantling procedure.

3 The counterweights of the automatic advance unit should return to their normal position with smooth action when they are spread apart with the fingers and released. A visual inspection will show signs of damage or broken springs.

4 It is unlikely that the automatic advance unit will need to be dismantled, unless replacement parts have to be fitted.

10 Sparking plug: checking and resetting gap

1 A 10 mm NGK sparking plug is fitted to all C50 and C70 models as standard, the grade depending on the model designation. Refer to the Specifications Section heading this Chapter for the recommended grades. The C90 model has a 12 mm plug.

2 All models use a sparking plug with a 12.7 mm reach which should be gapped at 0.024 in. Always use the grade of plug recommended or the exact equivalent in another manufacturer's range.

3 Check the gap at the plug points during every six monthly or 3,000 mile service. To reset the gap, bend the outer electrode to bring it closer to the central electrode and check that a 0.024 inch feeler blade can be inserted. Never bend the central electrode, otherwise the insulator will crack, causing engine damage if particles fall in whilst the engine is running.

4 The condition of the sparking plug electrodes and insulator can be used as a reliable guide to engine operating conditions. See accompanying diagrams.

5 Always carry a spare sparking plug of the correct grade. In the rare event of plug failure it will enable the engine to be restarted.

6 Never over-tighten a sparking plug, otherwise there is risk of stripping the threads from the cylinder head, particularly those cast in light alloy. The plug should be sufficiently tight to seat firmly on the copper sealing washer. Use a spanner that is a good fit, otherwise the spanner may slip and break the insulator.

7 Make sure the plug insulating cap is a good fit and free from cracks. This cap contains the suppressor that eliminates radio and TV interference.

11 Fault diagnosis: ignition system

Symptom	Cause	Remedy
Engine will not start	No spark at plug	Try replacement plug if gap correct. Check whether contact breaker points are opening and closing, also whether they are clean. Check whether points arc when separated. If so, renew condenser. Check ignition switch and ignition coil. Battery discharged. Switch off all lights and use emergency start.
Engine starts but runs erratically	Intermittent or weak spark	Try replacement plug. Check whether points are arcing. If so, replace condenser. Check accuracy of ignition timing. Low output from flywheel magneto generator, or imminent breakdown of ignition coil.
	Automatic advance unit stuck or damaged	Check unit for freedom of action and broken springs.

Chapter 5 Frame and forks

Contents

Specifications

Frame	Spine type, scooter style
Front suspension	Hydraulically damped leading link forks
Rear suspension	Pressed steel swinging arm controlled by hydraulically damped suspension units
Caster angle	63°
Trail	75 mm (2.95 inch)
Maximum lock	45° C50 and C70 models 43° C90 model

1 General description

The frame used on these models is of the scooter style spine type ie. it has a single tube holding the steering head mounted low enough to step over. This is why the models are sometimes referred to as step-thru models. The forks are of the leading link variety, with hydraulic damping. The rear suspension is of the swinging arm type, controlled by two suspension units also with hydraulic damping.

The C70 model has, in addition to the normal centre stand, a prop stand mounted on the footrest bar.

2 Front forks: removal from frame

1 It is extremely unlikely that the front forks will need to be removed from the frame as a unit unless the steering head bearings give trouble or the forks are damaged in an accident.
2 Commence operations by placing the machine on the centre stand.
3 Remove the front wheel as described in Chapter 6.3.
4 Although not essential, it is advisable to remove the front mudguard for ease of handling. Remove the two self-locking nuts and their washers and the two upper fixing bolts and

2.4a Remove the self-locking nuts ...

2.4b ... and the bolts to release the mudguard

Fig. 5.1. Handlebar assembly - C70 model

1	Throttle cable	11	Plug	20	Sliding block
2	Earth wire	12	Fork top plate	21	Cable stop
3	Earth wire	13	Handlebar assembly	22	Rubber grip
4	Bulb (2 off)	14	Handlebar assembly	23	Rubber grip
5	Speedometer assembly	15	Handlebar assembly	24	Fork top bridge
6	Speedometer assembly	16	Bottom cover	25	Top bridge rubber
7	Speedometer assembly	17	Bottom cover	26	Top bridge rubber
8	Spring	18	Rubber ring	27	Spacer
9	Return spring	19	Twistgrip sleeve	28	Top bridge plate
10	Front brake cable				

29	Spacer (2 off)
30	Label
31	Bolt (2 off)
32	Special nut
33	Special nut
34	Cup washer (2 off)
35	Washer (2 off)
36	Nut (2 off)
37	Washer (2 off)

washers. Pull the mudguard off the pivot bolts and clear of the machine, ensuring that the front brake and speedometer cables slide out of the moulded slot.

5   Remove the two bolts and the headlamp unit. Disconnect the headlamp wires and put the headlamp in a safe place.

6   Unscrew the top of the carburettor and disconnect the cable by unhooking the throttle slide and pulling off the carburettor components.

7   Remove the two nuts and their washers from the underside of the handlebar fairing. The handlebars can now be eased up to allow the remainder of the wires to be disconnected at their snap connectors. All the wires are colour coded, to make re-connection easy. The handlebars, complete with the fairing, speedometer and cables, can now be pulled clear.

8   Remove the two bolts and lockwashers and the slotted nut to release the top bridge plate. Remove the plate, the spacers, and the top mounting rubber. The top bridge will now slide off. The handlebar lower cover with its sealing ring can be lifted clear. The lower mounting rubber can be removed and the two 8 mm bolts, which will permit the fork top plate to be removed.

9   Support the fork legs, to prevent them dropping prematurely, and remove the steering head column nut.

10 Remove the top cone to reveal 21 ball bearings in the top race, which can then be lifted out with a magnet or a greased screwdriver.

11 As the forks are now lowered, the 21 ball bearings in the lower race will be displaced and once these have been collected, the fork assembly can be pulled clear of the frame.

12 The bottom cone, the dust seal and the dust seal holder, can be removed from the fork assembly, if required.

3   Front forks: dismantling

1   If only the fork leading links and suspension units are to be removed, without disturbing the head races, remove the front wheel as described in Chapter 6.3 and the self-locking nut and washer that retains the bottom of the mudguard.

2   Continue from here for further dismantling, irrespective of whether the forks are on or off the machine. Remove the bottom pivot bolt that was fitted with the self-locking nut. Remove the spring clip, the nut, the cup washer and the rubber washer, from the top of the suspension unit, and pull the link and suspension unit out of the forks.

3   The rubber rebound stop need not be removed unless it is damaged or perished, in which case it can be withdrawn by removing the nut and bolt that passes through it.

2.7a Remove the two nuts and washers ...

2.7b ... and lift handlebars partly off

3.2a Remove rearmost bolt to release leading link ...

3.2b ... and the spring clip, nut and washer to release the suspension unit

Fig. 5.2. Steering head assembly - C70 model

1	Reflector (2 off)	12	Bottom cone	23	Top cover
2	Setting piece (2 off)	13	Adjusting nut	24	Beading
3	Reflector base (2 off)	14	Steering lock	25	Beading
4	Resistor assembly	15	Front mudguard	26	Emblem
5	Mounting plate	16	Front mudguard	27	Screw (2 off)
6	Ball race cup (2 off)	17	Spacer (2 off)	28	Self-locking nut (2 off)
7	Front fork	18	Front number plate*	29	Bolt (2 off)
8	Blanking cap (2 off)	19	Nut plate (2 off)	30	Bolt (2 off)
9	Dust seal	20	Spacer (2 off)	31	Bolt (2 off)
10	Dust seal washer	21	Cover	32	Screw (4 off)
11	Top cone	22	Top cover	33	Screw

34	Screw
35	Screw
36	Nut
37	Nut
38	Washer (4 off)
39	Washer (3 off)
40	Washer (2 off)
41	Washer
42	Washer
43	Ball bearing (42 off)

* not required on UK models

Fig. 5.3. Front suspension - C70 model

1	Right-hand leading link	10 Dust seal cap (4 off)	18 Tapped spring register
2	Bush (2 off)	11 Rebound stop (2 off)	(2 off)
3	Bush (2 off)	12 Front shock absorber	19 Spacer (2 off)
4	Left-hand leading link	assembly (2 off)	20 Cup washer (2 off)
5	Spacer (2 off)	13 Spring (2 off)	21 Rubber mount (2 off)
6	Dust seal (4 off)	14 Spring register (2 off)	22 Rubber ring (2 off)
7	Dust seal cap (4 off)	15 Spring guide (2 off)	23 Spacer (2 off)
8	Spacer (2 off)	16 Damper assembly (2 off)	24 Bolt (2 off)
9	Dust seal (4 off)	17 Rubber stop (2 off)	

25 Bolt (2 off)
26 Nut (2 off)
27 Bolt (2 off)
28 Nut (2 off)
29 Nut (2 off)
30 Washer (2 off)
31 Spring clip (2 off)
32 Grease nipple (4 off)

3.4 Remove the pivot bolt to release the link

3.6 Dust cap and felt washer seal the bearing

4   To detach the bottom link from the suspension unit, remove the pivot bolt and nut.

5   If play is evident between any of the pivot pins and their respective bushes, both components will need to be renewed.

6   The dust seals and covers will need to be removed to gain access to the bushes and where the arm is peened over to retain the cover, care should be taken not to destroy the latter.

7   The bush is a press fit in the pivot eye, and the new bush can be used to press out the old one.

8   The suspension units can be dismantled partially if it is desired to remove the spring. Pull off the rubber disc and the spacer, unscrew the threaded spring register and remove the spring, the rubber stop, the spring guide, the thrust washer and the spacing collar. Renew the spring if it is below 120 mm (4.72 in) in length.

9   Note that the damper units are sealed and cannot be dismantled further. If the units leak or if the damping action is lost, replacement of the unit is the only satisfactory answer.

---

4   Steering head bearings: examination and renovation

---

1   Before commencing to reassemble the forks, inspect the steering head races. The ball bearing tracks should be polished and free from indentations or cracks. If signs of wear or damage are evident, the cups and cones must be replaced. They are a tight push fit and need to be drifted out of position.

2   Ball bearings are cheap. Each race has 21 x 6 mm ball bearings, which should be renewed if the originals are marked or discoloured. To hold the steel balls in position during the re-attachment of the forks, pack the bearings with grease.

3   The forks are reassembled and attached to the frame by following a reversal of the dismantling procedure. Do not over-tighten the steering head bearings, otherwise the handling characteristics of the machine will be affected. It is possible to over-tighten and create a load of several tons on the steering head bearings, even though the handlebars appear to turn with relative ease. As a guide, only very slight pressure should be needed to start the front wheel turning to either side under its own weight, when it is raised clear of the ground. Check also that the bearings are not too slack; there should be no discernable movement of the forks, in the fore and aft direction.

5.1 Steering lock is mounted under steering head

7.5 Rubber bushes can be driven out, if perished

5 Steering head lock

A steering head lock is attached to the lower fork yoke by two crosshead screws. The tongue of the lock engages with a hole drilled in a plate attached to the steering head column, so that the machine can be left unattended with the handlebars on full left lock. If the lock malfunctions, it must be replaced.

6 Frame assembly: inspection and renovation

1 The frame assembly is unlikely to require attention unless it has been damaged in an accident. Replacement of the complete unit is the only satisfactory course of action when the frame is out of alignment, if only because the special jigs and mandrels essential for resetting the frame will not be available.
2 After a machine has covered an extensive mileage, it is advisable to inspect the frame for signs of cracking or splitting in the vicinity of the engine mounting points. Repairs can be effected by welding.
3 Frame alignment should be checked when the machine is complete. The accompanying diagram shows how a board placed each side of the rear wheel can be used as a guide to alignment. It is, of course, necessary to ensure that both wheels are centrally disposed within their respective forks before carrying out this check.

7 Swinging arm rear fork: dismantling, inspection and reassembly

1 The rear fork of the frame assembly pivots on the rear fork pivot bolt which is carried in rubber bushes. Its action is controlled by two hydraulically-damped rear suspension units that each carry a compression spring, connected between the swinging arm fork and the frame, one on each side of the machine.
2 To detach the rear fork, remove the rear wheel, as described in Chapter 6.9. Remove the upper and lower halve of the rear chaincase and remove the final drive chain. Remove the final drive sprocket as described in Chapter 6.12.
3 Unscrew the 10 mm nut attaching each of the rear suspension units to the frame. Remove the domed nut that secures the lower eye of each unit to the swinging arm fork.
4 Unscrew the rear fork pivot nut and withdraw the fork pivot bolt. The swinging arm fork can now be removed from the frame.
5 Check the condition of the rubber bushes in the swinging arm fork pivot. A rubber bonded bush is fitted to each side, which can be pressed out if renewal is necessary. Replace the bushes if they show signs of damage or ageing, or if the pivot bolt is a slack fit. Check also the pivot bolt.
6 Place a straight metal rod across the open ends of the swinging arm fork, where the rear wheel spindle is normally located. Check for twist or deformation. If the amount of twist is more than 1 mm, the swinging arm fork should be replaced. A twisted rear fork will throw the wheels out of track and give the machine poor handling characteristics.
7 To reassemble the swinging arm fork assembly, reverse the procedure detailed above.

8 Rear suspension units: dismantling and inspection

1 The rear suspension units can be partially dismantled to gain access to the springs. Unscrew the upper eye of the unit from the damper rod after slackening the locknut. When the pivot eye has been removed, the top shroud can be pulled off and the spring and spring guide detached. If the free length of the spring is below 200 mm, it must be renewed.
2 If the suspension units show signs of leakage or if the damping action is no longer evident, the units should be renewed. Always renew both, as a matched pair, in the interests of good roadholding. The damper unit is sealed and cannot be repaired.

9 Centre stand and prop stand: inspection

1 The centre stand is attached to the lower extremities of the frame unit, to provide a convenient means of parking the machine on level ground. It pivots on the hollow tube that carries the rear brake pedal, which is retained in position by a split pin. A return spring retracts the stand when the machine is pushed forward, so that it can be wheeled prior to riding.
2 On the C70 model there is a prop stand fitted onto the footrest bar, also with a return spring.
3 The condition of the return springs and their return action should be checked regularly. If a stand falls whilst the machine is in motion, it may catch in some obstacle in the road and unseat the rider.

Fig. 5.4. Checking wheel alignment

A and C — Incorrect
B — Correct

9.2 Check the condition of the prop stand spring

Fig. 5.5. Swinging arm and chaincase - C70 model

1	Upper half of chaincase	9	Anchor arm
2	Bottom half of chaincase	10	Spring
3	Chain	11	Pillion footrest (2 off)
4	Spring link	12	Footrest rubber (2 off)
5	Chain adjuster	13	Swinging arm assembly
6	Chain adjuster	14	Blanking cap (2 off)
7	Blanking cap	15	Rubber bush (2 off)
8	Protection strip	16	Label

17	Label
18	Spindle bolt
19	Spindle bolt
20	Shouldered bolt
21	Bolt (3 off)
22	Bolt
23	Nut (2 off)
24	Nut (2 off)

25	Self-locking nut
26	Washer (6 off)
27	Washer (2 off)
28	Washer (2 off)
29	Washer
30	Split pin
31	Spring clip

Fig. 5.6. Rear suspension units - C70 model

1	Suspension unit assembly (2 off)	9	Lock nut (2 off)
2	Spring (2 off)	10	Rubber bush (2 off)
3	Spring guide (2 off)	11	Spacer (2 off)
4	Eye end (2 off)	12	Rubber bush (2 off)
5	Top spring cover (2 off)	13	Spacer (2 off)
6	Bottom spring cover (2 off)	14	Washer (4 off)
7	Damper assembly (2 off)	15	Washer (2 off)
8	Rubber stop (2 off)	16	Acorn nut (4 off)
		17	Washer (2 off)

10.1 Four bolts hold the footrest bar

13.1 Two nuts hold the dual seat

10 Footrests: inspection and renovation

1   The footrest bar is attached to the bottom of the crankcase of the engine unit by four 8 mm bolts and washers. The bar is malleable and is likely to become bent if the machine is dropped.
2   To straighten the bar first remove it from the machine and detach the footrest rubbers. It can then be bent straight in a vice, using a blow lamp to warm the tube if the bend is severe. Never attempt to straighten the bar whilst it is still attached to the crankcase, otherwise serious damage to the crankcase casting may result.

11 Speedometer: removal and replacement

1   A speedometer of the magnetic type is fitted to these Honda models. It contains also the odometer for recording the total mileage covered by the machine, a small bulb for illuminating the dial during the hours of darkness, and the neutral indicator lamp.
2   The speedometer is held in position by a tension spring. To remove the speedometer, remove the two bolts and the headlamp unit, and remove the two nuts and washers from the underside

of the handlebar fairing. Ease the cables into the fairing and lift the fairing sufficiently to unscrew the speedometer cable. Ease the fairing higher and release the clip that holds the speedometer head. The speedometer can now be lifted clear, from the top.
3   Although a speedometer on a machine of less than 100 cc capacity is not a statutory requirement in the UK, if one is fitted it must be in good working order. Reference to the mileage reading shown on the odometer is a good way of keeping in pace with the routine maintenance schedules.
4   Apart from defects in the speedometer drive or in the drive cable itself, a speedometer that malfunctions is difficult to repair. Fit a replacement or alternatively entrust the repair to an instrument repair specialist.

12 Speedometer cable: inspection and maintenance

1   It is advisable to detach the speedometer drive cable from time to time, in order to check whether it is adequately lubricated and whether the outer covering is compressed or damaged at any point along its run. A jerky or sluggish speedometer movement can often be attributed to a cable fault.
2   To grease the cable, withdraw the inner cable. After removing the old grease, clean with a petrol soaked rag and examine the cable for broken strands or other damage.
3   Re-grease the cable with high melting point grease, taking care not to grease the last six inches at the point where the cable enters the speedometer head. If this precaution is not observed, grease will work into the speedometer head and immobilise the movement.
4   If the speedometer and the odometer stop working, it is probable that the speedometer cable has broken. Inspection will show whether the inner cable has broken; if so, the inner cable alone can be renewed and reinserted in the outer covering after greasing. Never fit a new inner cable alone if the outer covering is damaged or compressed at any point along its run.

13 Dualseat: removal

1   The dualseat is removed by unscrewing the two bolts in the base of the seat, at the rear.
2   When the seat has been detached, the long bolt through the rear of the carrier can be removed.

14 Cleaning the plastic mouldings

1   The moulded plastic cycle parts, such as the front mudguard, and legshield cover will not respond to cleaning in the same way as the other metal parts as they are moulded in rigid polyethylene. It is best to wash these parts with a household detergent solution, which will remove oil and grease in a most effective manner.
2   Avoid the use of scouring powder as much as possible because this will score the surface of the mouldings and make them more receptive to dirt.

15 Cleaning: general

1   After removing all surface dirt with a rag or sponge that is washed frequently in clean water, the application of car polish or wax will give a good finish to the cycle parts of the machine, after they have dried thoroughly. The plated parts should require only a wipe over with a damp rag.
2   If possible, the machine should be wiped over immediately after it has been used in the wet, so that it is not garaged in damp conditions that will promote rusting. Make sure to wipe the chain and if necessary re-oil it, to prevent water from entering the rollers and causing harshness with an accompanying rapid rate of wear. Remember there is little chance of water entering the control cables if they are lubricated regularly, as recommended in the Routine Maintenance Section.

16 Fault diagnosis: Frame and fork assembly

Symptom	Cause	Remedy
Machine is unduly sensitive to road surface irregularities	Fork and/or rear suspension units damping ineffective ive	Renew suspension unit.
Machine rolls at low speeds	Steering head bearings overtight or damaged	Slacken bearing adjustment. If no improvement, dismantle and inspect head bearings.
Machine tends to wander; steering is imprecise	Worn swinging arm suspension bearings	Check and if necessary renew pivot bolt and bushes.
Fork action stiff	Fork legs have twisted	Check alignment.
Forks judder when front brake is applied	Worn bushes in fork assembly Steering head bearings too slack	Strip forks and renew bushes. Readjust to take up play.
Wheels seem out of alignment	Frame distorted as result of accident damage	Check frame after stripping out. If bent, replacement frame is necessary.

Chapter 6 Wheels, brakes and tyres

Contents

Specifications

Wheels	17 inch diameter front and rear
Tyres	2.25 inch x 17 inch front and rear (C50 and C70 models)
	2.50 inch x 17 inch front and rear (C90 model)

Tyre pressures

Front	26 psi (1.8 kg/cm^2)
Rear solo	29 psi (2.0 kg/cm^2)
with pillion	32 psi (2.2 kg/cm^2)

Brakes	Internally expanding 110 mm diameter front and rear
Chain size	½ inch x ¼ inch all models
Chain length	98 links (C50 and C70 models)
	100 links (C90 model)
Engine sprocket	13 teeth (C50 model)
	14 teeth (C70 and C90 models)
Rear wheel sprocket	41 teeth (C50 model)
	39 teeth (C70 model)
	40 teeth (C90 model)

---

1 General description

Both wheels are of 17 inch diameter and carry tyres of 2.25
inch section (2.50 inch section, 90 cc models), a ribbed tyre at
the front and a block tread at the rear. Steel wheel rims are
used in conjunction with cast aluminium alloy hubs, each hub
containing a 110 mm internal expanding brake. The wheels are
not interchangeable because the rear wheel incorporates a special
cush drive arrangement to act as a transmission shock absorber.
Both wheels are quickly detachable; the rear wheel can be
removed from the frame without disturbing the rear wheel
sprocket or the final drive chain.

2 Front wheel: examination and renovation

1 Place the machine on the centre stand so that the front wheel
is raised clear of the ground. Spin the wheel and check for rim
alignment or run-out. Small irregularities can be corrected by
tightening the spokes in the area affected, although a certain
amount of experience is advisable if over-correction is to be
avoided.
2 Any flats in the wheel rim should be evident at the same
time. These are much more difficult to remove and in most cases
the wheel will need to be rebuilt on a new rim. Apart from the
effect on stability, there is greater risk of damage to the tyre

bead and walls if the machine is run with a deformed wheel. In an extreme case the tyre can even separate from the rim.

3   Check for loose or broken spokes. Tapping the spokes is the best guide to tension. A loose spoke will produce a quite different sound and should be tightened by turning the nipple in an anticlockwise direction. Always recheck for run-out by spinning the wheel again.

4   If it is necessary to turn a spoke nipple an excessive amount to restore tension, it is advisable to remove the tyre and tube so that the end of the spoke that now protrudes into the wheel rim can be ground flush. If this precaution is not taken, there is danger of the spoke end chafing the inner tube and causing an eventual puncture.

3   Front wheel: removal

1   Commence operations by placing the machine on the centre stand, on level ground.

2   Disconnect the speedometer cable by unscrewing it from the brake backplate and disconnect the front brake cable.

3   On the early C90 models there is a separate torque arm, which needs to be disconnected.

4   Withdraw the split pin from the front wheel spindle nut and remove the nut and washer. The front wheel spindle can now be pulled out, releasing the wheel complete with brake assembly. Ensure that the machine is well supported so that it does not topple forward once the wheel is removed.

4   Front brake assembly: examination, renovation and reassembly

1   To remove the brake assembly, the backplate lifts straight out of the brake drum.

2   Examine the brake linings. If they are wearing thin or unevenly, the brake shoes should be renewed. The linings are bonded on and cannot be replaced as a separate item.

3   To remove the brake shoes from the brake plate assembly, arrange the operating lever so that the brakes are in the 'full on' position and then pull the shoes apart whilst lifting them upward in the form of a 'V'. When they are clear of the brake plate, the return springs can be removed and the shoes separated.

4   Before replacing the brake shoes, check that the brake operating cam is working smoothly and is not binding in its pivot. The cam can be removed by withdrawing the retaining nut on the operating arm and pulling the arm off the shaft. Before

2.1 Badly buckled wheel rim

3.2 Disconnect the speedometer and brake cables

3.3 Early models have an anchor arm

4.1 The brake assembly lifts out of the drum

Fig. 6.1. Front wheel assembly - C90 model

1	Wheel rim	11	Speedometer gear	21	Dust seal	31	Washer
2	Spindle	12	Speedometer cable	22	Rubber bush (2 off)	32	Washer (2 off)
3	Spacer	13	Speedometer cable	23	Brake lever arm	33	Washer
4	Wheel hub	14	Brake backplate	24	Brake arm return spring	34	Oil seal
5	Spoke (18 off)	15	Brake shoe (2 off)	25	Anchor arm	35	Oil seal
6	Bearing spacer	16	Operating cam	26	Special nut	36	Bolt
7	Spoke (18 off)	17	Brake shoe spring (2 off)	27	Bolt	37	Ball bearing (2 off)
8	Tyre	18	Dust seal	28	Bolt	38	Grease nipple
9	Inner tube	19	Spacer	29	Spindle nut		
10	Rim tape	20	Dust seal cap	30	Self-locking nut (2 off)		

removing the arm, it is advisable to mark its position in relation to the shaft, so that it can be relocated correctly. The shaft should be greased prior to reassembly and also a light smear of grease placed on the faces of the operating cam.

5   Check the inner surface of the brake drum on which the brake shoes bear. The surface should be smooth and free from score marks or indentations, otherwise reduced braking efficiency will be inevitable. Remove all traces of brake lining dust and wipe with a clean rag soaked in petrol to remove any traces of grease or oil.

6   If the brake drum has become scored, special attention is required. It is possible to skim a brake drum in a lathe provided the score marks are not too deep. Under these circumstances, packing will have to be added to the ends of the brake shoes, to compensate for the amount of metal removed from the surface of the drum.

7   To reassemble the brake shoes on the brake plate, fit the return springs first and then force the shoes apart, holding them in a 'V' formation. If they are now located with the brake operating cam and pivot they can usually be snapped into position by pressing downward. Never use excessive force, otherwise there is risk of distorting the shoes permanently.

4.4 Punch marks on brake lever and operating spindle allow correct reassembly

---

5   Front wheel bearings: examination and replacement

1   The front wheel bearings are of the ball journal type and are not adjustable. If the bearings are worn, indicated by side play at the wheel rim, the bearings must be renewed.

2   Access to the wheel bearings is gained when the brake plate has been removed from the front wheel. There is an oil seal in front of the bearing on the brake drum side, to prevent grease from reaching the brake operating parts. This seal should be prised out of position and a new replacement obtained.

3   The wheel bearings are a drive fit in the hub. Use a double diameter drift to displace the bearings from the hub, working from each side of the hub. When the first bearing emerges from the hub the hollow distance collar that separates them can be removed.

4   Remove all the old grease from the hub and bearings, giving the latter a final wash in petrol. Check the bearings for play or signs of roughness when they are turned. If there is any doubt about their condition, renew them.

5   Before replacing the bearings, first pack the hub with new grease. Then grease both bearings and drive them back into position with the same double diameter drift, not forgetting the

4.5 Clean the brake drum to remove any dust

4.7 Snap brake shoes back into position, as shown

5.3 Use a suitable drift for removing and replacing bearings

5.5a Refit the new bearings ...

5.5b ... and use care when fitting the oil seal

6.4 Small screw retains worm gear

6.5 Speedometer drive gear tongues engage with slots in hub

9.1a Remove the spring clip and nut ...

9.1b ... and pull the anchor arm free

distance collar that separates them. Fit the replacement oil seals in front of the bearing on the brake drum side.

6 Speedometer drive gears: examination and replacement

1   The speedometer drive gears are housed in the front brake backplate and are driven by two tongues that engage with slots in the hub.
2   The drive gears should be checked for wear or broken teeth and renewed if necessary.
3   The large gear with its two drive tongues simply lifts out of the backplate.
4   To renew the small worm gear it is necessary to remove the very small screw before prising it out, together with its bushes.
5   Reassembly of the gears is by reversing the above procedure, ensuring that the gear tongues engage with the hub slots. Thoroughly grease the gears and ensure that the oil seal is in good condition.

7 Front wheel: replacement

1   To replace the front wheel, reverse the removal procedure and ensure that the peg on the forks locates in the slot in the brakeplate, or the anchor arm is fixed securely. This cannot be overstressed as failure to anchor the brakeplate will cause the brake to lock on when it is first applied.
2   Reconnect the front brake and check that the brake functions correctly, especially if the adjustment has been altered or the brake operating arm has been removed and replaced during the dismantling operation.
3   Reconnect the speedometer drive.
4   On early C90 models do not omit to replace and tighten the torque arm.

8 Rear wheel: examination and renovation

1   Place the machine on the centre stand, so that the rear wheel is clear of the ground. Check the wheel for rim alignment, damage to the rim or loose or broken spokes, by following the procedure adopted for the front wheel in Section 2 of this Chapter.

9 Rear wheel: removal

1   To remove the rear wheel, place the machine on the centre stand so that the wheel is raised clear of the ground. Remove the brake adjusting nut and separate the brake rod from the operating arm of the rear brake. Remove the clip, slacken and remove the nut and bolt from the rear brake torque arm, at the brake plate anchorage.
2   Remove the split pin, the centre of the two rear wheel spindle nuts and pull the spindle from the hub. Remove the distance pieces if they have not fallen clear and disengage the hub from the cush drive assembly by pulling the wheel towards the right-hand side of the machine. The wheel can now be removed from the frame complete with the rear brake assembly, leaving the rear sprocket and final drive chain in position.

10 Rear brake assembly: examination, renovation and reassembly

As the rear brake is identical to the front brake, the advice given in Section 4 of this Chapter will apply.

11 Rear wheel bearings: examination and replacement

As the bearing layout for the hubs is identical, the procedure

9.2 Pull out the spindle and remove the spacer

12.3 Remove the nut to release the sprocket assembly

described in Section 5 of this Chapter will apply for each model.

12 Rear wheel sprocket: removal, examination and replacement

1   It is unlikely that the sprocket will require renewal until a very substantial mileage has been covered. The usual signs of wear occur when the teeth assume a hooked or very shallow formation that will cause rapid wear of the chain. A worn sprocket must be renewed, together with the gearbox final drive sprocket and the chain. Always renew the final drive assembly as a complete set, otherwise rapid wear will occur as the result of running old and new parts together.
2   As the sprocket is left attached to the machine when the rear wheel is removed, the chainguard halves must be removed for access. Remove the two bolts on each half and pull the top half clear first.
3   Disconnect the chain at the spring link and pull it clear of the rear sprocket. Remove the stub axle nut and washer and pull the sprocket assembly clear of the machine. Prise down the two double tab washers, remove the four fixing bolts and lift the sprocket off.
4   To refit the sprocket, reverse the dismantling procedure.

Fig. 6.2. Rear wheel assembly - C90 model

1	Sprocket	9	Bearing spacer	18	Inner tube	27	Oil seal
2	Shock absorber rubber	10	Spoke (18 off)	19	Rim tape	28	Bolt
	(4 off)	11	O-ring	20	Brake shoe (2 off)	29	Bolt
3	Wheel spindle	12	Wheel rim	21	Brake shoe spring (2 off)	30	Nut
4	Stub axle	13	Tyre	22	Bolt (4 off)	31	Nut (4 off)
5	Spacer	14	Spoke (18 off)	23	Spindle nut	32	Split pin
6	Spacer	15	Brake backplate	24	Stub axle nut	33	Ball bearing
7	Wheel hub	16	Operating cam	25	Tab washer (2 off)	34	Ball bearing
8	Shock absorber hub	17	Brake lever arm	26	Washer (2 off)	35	Ball bearing

13 Rear wheel shock absorber assembly: examination and replacement

1 The shock absorber assembly is removed from the machine as described in the preceding Section.
2 The shock absorber assembly has a ball journal bearing and if worn the following procedure should be followed.
3 Tap out the stub axle, remove the spacer from the centre of the oil seal, prise out the oil seal and drive the bearing out of the housing.
4 To replace the bearing, reverse the above procedure, ensuring that the bearing is well greased and the oil seal is in good condition.
5 The shock absorber rubbers should be checked for any damage or deterioration. All oil or grease should be wiped away as this may cause premature deterioration.
6 To refit the shock absorber assembly reverse the dismantling procedure described in Sections 9 and 12.

14 Rear wheel: reassembly

1 To refit the rear wheel, reverse the removal procedure, ensuring that the brake anchor arm is securely fitted. If the anchor arm becomes detached, the rear brake will lock in the pull-on position immediately it is applied and may give rise to a serious accident.
2 Before fully tightening all the nuts, ensure that the final chain tension and the brake adjustment is correct.
3 Check also whether the wheel alignment is correct as described in Chapter 5, Section 6, paragraph 3.
4 Do not omit to replace the split pin that passes through the rear wheel spindle nut.

15 Front and rear brakes: adjustment

1 The front brake adjuster is located on the front brake cable. The brake should be adjusted so that the wheel is free to revolve before pressure is applied to the handlebar lever, and is applied fully before the handlebar lever touches the handlebar.
2 The rear brake is adjusted by means of the adjusting nut on the end of the brake cable or rod. Adjustment is largely a matter of personal choice, but excessive travel of the footbrake pedal should not be necessary before the brake is applied fully.

13.3 Remove the stub axle

13.4a Refit the new bearing ...

13.4b ... and refit the oil seal

13.5 Check the condition of the cush drive rubbers

16.2 Check for correct chain tension in middle of bottom run

16.5 There is a chain of British manufacture available when renewal is necessary

16.7 Ensure that the spring clip is fitted the correct way round

3 Efficient brakes depend on good leverage of the operating arm. The angle between the brake operating arm and the cable or rod should never exceed 90° when the brake is fully applied.
4 Check that the brakes pull off correctly when the lever and pedal are released. Sluggish action can usually be traced to a broken return spring on the brake shoes or a tendency for the operating cam to bind in its bush.

16 Final drive chain: examination and lubrication

1 The final drive chain is fully enclosed within a chaincase. Periodically, the tension of the chain will need to be adjusted, to compensate for wear. This is accomplished by sliding the rear wheel backwards in the ends of the rear fork, using the drawbolt adjusters provided. The rear wheel spindle nuts must be slackened before the drawbolts can be turned; also the torque arm bolt on the rear brake plate.
2 The chain is in correct adjustment if there is from 1 - 2 cm free play in the middle of the lower run. An inspection plug in the lower section of the full chaincase permits access to the chain to check whether the tension is correct.
3 Always adjust the chain adjusters an identical amount, otherwise the rear wheel will be thrown out of alignment. If in doubt about the correctness of wheel alignment, use the technique described in Chapter 5, Section 6, paragraph 3.
4 After a period of running, the chain will require lubrication. Lack of oil will accelerate the rate of wear of both chain and sprockets, leading to harsh transmission. The application of engine oil from an oil can will serve as a satisfactory lubricant, but it is preferable to remove the chain at regular intervals and immerse it in a molten lubricant such as Linklyfe, after it has been cleaned in a paraffin bath. This latter type of lubricant achieves better penetration of the chain links and rollers and is less likely to be thrown off when the chain is in motion. An equally effective and less messy alternative is a spray-on lubricant of the aerosol type, such as Castrol Chain Lubricant.
5 The chain fitted as standard is of Japanese manufacture. When renewal is necessary, it should be noted that a Renold equivalent of British manufacture is available as an alternative. The size and length of chain is stated in the Specifications Section.
6 To check whether the chain requires replacement, lay it lengthwise in a straight line and compress it so that all play is taken up. Anchor one end and then pull on the other end to take up the end play in the other direction. If the chain extends by more than the distance between two adjacent rollers, it should be renewed in conjunction with the two sprockets. Note that this check should be made after the chain has been washed but before any lubricant is applied, otherwise the lubricant will take up some of the play.
7 When replacing the chain, make sure the spring link is correctly seated, with the closed end facing the direction of travel. Also make sure the chaincase is firmly secured.

17 Tyres: removal and replacement

1 At some time or other the need will arise to remove and replace the tyres, either as the result of a puncture or because a replacement is required to offset wear. To the inexperienced, tyre changing represents a formidable task, yet if a few simple rules are observed and the technique learned, the whole operation is surprisingly simple.
2 To remove the tyre from either wheel, first detach the wheel from the machine by following the procedure in Sections 3 or 9, depending on whether the front or the rear wheel is involved. Deflate the tyre by removing the valve insert and when it is fully deflated, push the bead of the tyre away from the wheel rim on both sides so that the bead enters the centre well of the rim. Remove the locking cap and push the tyre valve into the tyre itself.
3 Insert a tyre lever close to the valve and lever the edge of the

Tyre changing sequence - tubed tyres

 A Deflate tyre. After pushing tyre beads away from rim flanges push tyre bead into well of rim at point opposite valve. Insert tyre lever adjacent to valve and work bead over edge of rim.

Use two levers to work bead over edge of rim. Note use of rim protectors **B**

 C Remove inner tube from tyre

When first bead is clear, remove tyre as shown **D**

 E When fitting, partially inflate inner tube and insert in tyre

Work first bead over rim and feed valve through hole in rim. Partially screw on retaining nut to hold valve in place. **F**

 G Check that inner tube is positioned correctly and work second bead over rim using tyre levers. Start at a point opposite valve.

Work final area of bead over rim whilst pushing valve inwards to ensure that inner tube is not trapped **H**

tyre over the outside of the wheel rim. Very little force should be necessary; if resistance is encountered it is probably due to the fact that the tyre beads have not entered the well of the wheel rim all the way round the tyre.

4 Once the tyre has been edged over the wheel rim, it is easy to work around the wheel rim so that the tyre is completely free on one side. At this stage, the inner tube can be removed.

5 Working from the other side of the wheel, ease the other edge of the tyre over the outside of the wheel rim that is furthest away. Continue to work around the rim until the tyre is free completely from the rim.

6 If a puncture has necessitated the removal of the tyre, re-inflate the inner tube and immerse it in a bowl of water to trace the source of the leak. Mark its position and deflate the tube. Dry the tube and clean the area around the puncture with a petrol-soaked rag. When the surface has dried, apply the rubber solution and allow this to dry before removing the backing from the patch and applying the patch to the surface.

7 It is best to use a patch of the self-vulcanising type, which will form a very permanent repair. Note that it may be necessary to remove a protective covering from the top surface of the patch after it has sealed in position. Inner tubes made from synthetic rubber may require a special type of patch and adhesive, if a satisfactory bond is to be achieved.

8 Before replacing the tyre, check the inside to make sure the agent that caused the puncture is not trapped. Check also the outside of the tyre, particularly the tread area, to make sure nothing is trapped that may cause a further puncture.

9 If the inner tube has been patched on a number of past occasions, or if there is a tear or large hole, it is preferable to discard it and fit a replacement. Sudden deflation may cause an accident, particularly if it occurs with the front wheel.

10 To replace the tyre, inflate the inner tube sufficiently for it to assume a circular shape but only just. Then push it into the tyre so that it is enclosed completely. Lay the tyre on the wheel at an angle and insert the valve through the rim tape and the hole in the wheel rim. Attach the locking cap on the first few threads, sufficient to hold the valve captive in its correct location.

11 Starting at the point furthest from the valve, push the tyre bead over the edge of the wheel rim until it is located in the central well. Continue to work around the tyre in this fashion until the whole of one side of the tyre is on the rim. It may be necessary to use a tyre lever during the final stages.

12 Make sure there is no pull on the tyre valve and again commencing with the area furthest from the valve, ease the other bead of the tyre over the edge of the rim. Finish with the area close to the valve, pushing the valve up into the tyre until the locking cap touches the rim. This will ensure the inner tube is not trapped when the last section of the bead is edged over the rim with a tyre lever.

13 Check that the inner tube is not trapped at any point. Re-inflate the inner tube, and check that the tyre is seating correctly around the wheel rim. There should be a thin rib moulded around the wall of the tyre on both sides, which should be equidistant from the wheel rim at all points. If the tyre is unevenly located on the rim, try bouncing the wheel when the tyre is at the recommended pressure. It is probable that one of the beads has not pulled clear of the centre well.

14 Always run the tyres at the recommended pressures and never under or over-inflate. The correct pressures for solo use are given in the Specifications Section of this Chapter. If a pillion passenger is carried, increase the rear tyre pressure only.

15 Tyre replacement is aided by dusting the side walls, particularly in the vicinity of the beads, with a liberal coating of french chalk. Washing-up liquid can also be used to good effect, but this has the disadvantage of causing the inner surfaces of the wheel rim to rust.

16 Never replace the inner tube and tyre without the rim tape in position. If this precaution is overlooked there is a good chance of the ends of the spoke nipples chafing the inner tube and causing a crop of punctures.

17 Never fit a tyre that has a damaged tread or side walls. Apart from the legal aspects, there is a very great risk of a blow-out, which can have serious consequences on any two-wheel vehicle.

18 Tyre valves rarely give trouble, but it is always advisable to check whether the valve itself is leaking before removing the tyre. Do not forget to fit the dust cap, which forms an effective second seal.

18 Fault diagnosis: wheels, brakes and tyres

Symptom	Cause	Remedy
Handlebars oscillate at low speeds	Buckle or flat in wheel rim, most probably front wheel	Check rim alignment by spinning wheel. Correct by retensioning spokes or by having wheel rebuilt on new rim.
	Tyre not straight on rim	Check tyre alignment.
Machine lacks power and accelerates poorly	Brakes binding	Warm brake drums provide best evidence. Re-adjust brakes.
Brakes grab when applied gently	Ends of brake shoes not chamfered	Chamfer with file.
	Elliptical brake drum	Lightly skim in lathe (specialist attention needed).
Brake pull-off sluggish	Brake cam binding in housing	Free and grease.
	Weak brake shoe springs	Renew if springs not displaced.
Harsh transmission	Worn or badly adjusted chain	Adjust or renew as necessary.
	Hooked or badly worn sprockets	Renew as a pair.
Tyres wear more rapidly in middle of tread	Over inflation	Check pressures and run at recommended settings.
Tyres wear rapidly at outer edges of tread	Under inflation	Ditto.

Chapter 7 Electrical system

Contents

Specifications

Battery

	C50	C70	C90
Type	Lead acid, 6 volt		
Make	Yuasa Denki	Yuasa Denki	Yuasa Denki
Capacity	4 amp hours	4 amp hours	5.5 amp hours
Earth lead	Negative	Negative	Negative
Fuse value	15 amp	15 amp	15 amp

Bulbs (all 6 volt)

	C50	C70	C90
Headlamp	15/15W (early) 25/25W (late)	25/25W	25/25W
Pilot lamp	N/App	5W	4W
Stop/tail lamp	18/5W (early) 21/5W (late)	21/5W	18/5W (early) 21/5W (late)
Speedometer and neutral indicator lamps	1.5W	1.5W	1.5W
Flashing indicator lamps	18W	18W	18W
Courtesy lamp	N/App	3W	N/App

1 General description

While all models are fitted with a 6 volt electrical system there are two distinct types. The C50 and C70 models share a similar system in which most of the remaining flywheel generator coil output is used to feed the lights when the engine is running. A second tap off the coil supplies an ac current which is converted to dc by a rectifier to charge the battery, this supplying the needs of the horn, stop lamp, flashing indicators and other electrical fittings. The C90 models are fitted with an ac generator (alternator), its output being converted to dc by a rectifier to charge the battery, which then supplies the current for all electrical equipment.

In both cases a form of voltage control is provided by routing the generator output (partially) through the lighting switch so that extra power is supplied when necessary.

2 Flywheel generators: checking the output

As explained in Chapter 4.2, the output from either type of generator can be checked only with specialised test equipment of the multi-meter type. If the generator is suspect, it should be checked by either a Honda agent or an auto-electrical expert.

3 Battery: inspection and maintenance

1 Two types of Yuasa battery having different amp hour capacities are fitted. The C50 and C70 models use a 4 amp hour battery, whilst the C90 uses a 6 amp hour battery.

2 The transparent case of the battery allows the upper and lower levels of the electrolyte to be observed without need to remove the battery. Batteries of the lead/acid type are employed.

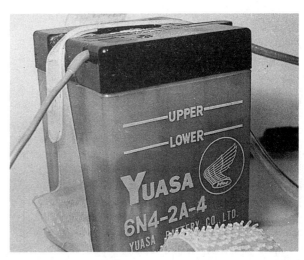

3.2 The acid level can be seen through the case

3.7 A single bolt retains the battery and carrier to the frame

5.2 The selenium rectifier is mounted by the battery

6.1 The fuse holder clips under the battery, and unscrews to release the fuse

Maintenance is normally limited to keeping the electrolyte level within the prescribed upper and lower limits and making sure that the vent tube is not blocked. The lead plates and their separators can also be seen through the transparent case, a further guide to the condition of the battery.

3   Unless acid is spilt, as may occur when the machine falls over, the electrolyte should always be topped up with distilled water, to restore the correct level. If acid is spilt on any part of the machine, it should be neutralised with an alkali such as washing soda and washed away with plenty of water, otherwise serious corrosion will occur. Top up with sulphuric acid of the correct specific gravity (1.260 - 1.280) only when spillage has occurred.

4   It is seldom practicable to repair a cracked case because the acid in the joint prevents the formation of an effective seal. It is always best to replace a cracked battery, especially in view of the corrosion that will be caused by the leakage of acid.

5   Never check the condition of a battery by shorting the terminals. The very heavy current flow resulting from this sudden discharge will cause the battery to overheat, with consequent damage to the plates and the compound they hold.

6   If the machine is laid up for any time, it is advisable to disconnect and remove the battery. It should not be allowed to discharge completely, otherwise sulphation is liable to occur, an irreversible change in the condition of the plates that will render the battery useless.

7   A single screw retains the battery carrier in position under the right-hand side cover.

4   Battery: charging procedure

1   Whilst the machine is running it is unlikely that the battery will require attention other than routine maintenance because the generator will keep it charged. However, if the machine is used for a succession of short journeys mainly during the hours of darkness when the lights are in full use, it is unlikely that the output from the generator will be able to keep pace with the heavy electrical demand. Under these circumstances it will be necessary to remove the battery from time to time, to have it recharged independently.

2   The normal charging rate for the two types of battery fitted to the Honda 50 cc and 90 cc models is 0.2 amps. A more rapid charge can be given in an emergency, in which case the charging rate can be raised to 0.6 - 1.0 amps. The higher charge rate should be avoided if possible because this will eventually shorten the working life of the battery.

3   When the battery has been removed from a machine that has been laid up, a 'refresher' charge should be given every six weeks if the battery is to be maintained in good condition.

5   Selenium rectifier: general description

1   The function of the selenium rectifier is to convert the a.c. produced by the generator to d.c. so that it can be used to charge the battery and operate the lighting circuit etc.

The C50 and C70 models have a half wave rectifier while the C90 model has a full wave rectifier.

2   The rectifier is located alongside the battery under the right-hand side cover. Apart from physical damage, the rectifier is unlikely to give trouble during normal service. It is not practicable to repair a damaged rectifier; replacement is the only satisfactory solution.

3   Damage to the rectifier is likely to occur, however, if the machine is run without the battery for any period of time. A high voltage will develop in the absence of any load on the coil, which will cause a reverse flow of current and consequent damage to the rectifier cells.

4   It is not possible to check whether the rectifier is functioning correctly without the appropriate test equipment. A Honda agent or an auto-electrical expert are best qualified to advise in such cases.

5   Do not loosen the rectifier locking nut (painted) or bend,

cut, scratch or rotate the selenium wafers. Any such action will cause the electrode alloy coating to peel and destroy the working action.

---

6 Fuse: location and replacement

1   A fuse is incorporated in the electrical system to give protection from a sudden overload, such as may occur during a short circuit. The fuse is located within the fuse holder attached to the positive lead of the battery. All models have a 15 amp fuse.

2   If a fuse blows it should be replaced, after checking to ensure that no obvious short circuit has occurred. If the second fuse blows shortly afterwards, the electrical circuit should be checked in order to trace the fault.

3   When a fuse blows whilst running the machine and no spare is available, a 'get you home' dodge is to remove the blown fuse and wrap it in silver paper before replacing it in the fuse holder. The silver paper will restore the electrical continuity by bridging the broken fuse wire. This expedient should never be used if there is evidence of a short circuit, otherwise more serious damage will be caused. Replace the blown fuse at the earliest possible opportunity, to restore the full circuit protection.

---

7 Headlamp: replacing bulb and adjusting beam height

1   To remove the headlamp unit, detach the two bolts that hold the unit to the bottom half of the handlebar fairing and pull the unit clear. To remove the bulb, unhook the spring and pull the bulb holder free, then remove the bulb from the holder.

2   A double filament 25/25 watt bulb is fitted on later models, 15/15 watt on early C50 models.

3   It is not necessary to refocus the headlamp when a new bulb is fitted because the bulbs used are of the pre-focus type. To release the bulb holder from the reflector, pull from the locating flange.

4   Beam height is adjusted by means of the small screw on the lamp rim. Adjustments should always be made with the rider normally seated.

UK lighting regulations stipulate that the lighting system must be arranged so that the light will not dazzle a person standing in the same horizontal plane as the vehicle at a distance greater than 25 yards from the lamp, whose eye level is not less than 3 feet 6 inches above that plane. It is easy to approximate

7.1a Remove the two headlamp retaining screws ...

7.1b ... and unclip the bulbholder to replace the bulb

7.4 The reflector unit pivots for adjusting beam height

8.1 Slacken two screws to remove lens cover

9.2 Remove two screws and plastic lens to replace bulb

10.1 The flasher unit is mounted by the battery

13.2 Remove two screws and the plastic lens to replace bulb

this setting by placing the machine 25 yards away from a wall, concentrating at the same height as the distance from the centre of the headlamp to the ground. The rider must be seated

normally during this operation and also the pillion passenger, if one is carried regularly.

8 Stop and tail lamp: replacing bulb

1 The rear lamp has a twin filament bulb to illuminate the rear of the machine and the rear number plate, and to give visual warning when the rear brake is applied. To gain access to the bulb, remove the two screws that retain the moulded plastic lens cover to the tail lamp assembly and remove the cover complete with sealing gasket.
2 If tail lamps keep blowing, suspect either vibration in the rear mudguard assembly, or a poor earth connection.
3 The stop lamp is operated by a stop lamp switch on the right-hand side of the machine, immediately above the rear brake pedal. It is connected to the pedal by a spring, which acts as the operating medium. The body of the stop lamp switch is threaded, so that a limited range of adjustment is provided to determine when the lamp will operate.

9 Flashing indicators: replacement of bulbs

1 The flashing indicators are located on the handlebar fairing. The rear-facing indicators are attached to the rear mudguard, below the seat or carrier.
2 In each case, access to the bulb is gained by removing the two screws and moulded plastic lens cover. Bulbs are rated at 18 watts.

10 Flasher unit: location and replacement

1 The flasher unit is located close to the battery, hanging vertically downwards from a single bolt fixing to the frame.
2 A series of audible clicks will be heard if the flasher unit is functioning correctly. If the unit malfunctions, the usual symptom is one initial flash before the unit goes dead. It will be necessary to replace the flasher unit complete if the fault cannot be attributed to either a burnt out indicator bulb or a blown fuse. Take care in handling the unit because it is easily damaged, if dropped.

11 Neutral indicator bulb: replacement

1 A neutral indicator light is incorporated in the speedometer, to show when the gear change lever is in neutral. A small contact in the gearbox selector drum provides the appropriate indication. Failure to indicate the selection of neutral can usually be attributed to a broken wire or a damaged contact.
2 The neutral indicator lamp is rated at 1.5W. It is a push fit into the rubber sleeve that holds it close to the green-coloured indicator glass.

12 Speedometer bulb: replacement

1 A 1.5W bulb is inserted from the bottom of the speedometer casing to illuminate the dial during the hours of darkness.

13 Pilot light bulb: replacement - C70 and C90 models only

1 The pilot light is mounted on the front cover, immediately below the headlight.
2 Access to the bulb is gained once the two screws and the moulded plastic cover have been removed. The bulb is rated at 5 watts.
3 On C90 models the bulb is rated at 4 watts and is pressed into a rubber grommet in the rear of the headlamp reflector.

14 Resistance unit: general description - C70 model only

1 A resistance unit is mounted alongside the air cleaner. Its function is to protect the bulbs from a surge of power when the engine is started, with the lighting switch in the 'P' position.
2 To remove the resistance unit, the legshield assembly must first be detached, the wires disconnected at the snap connectors and the central mounting nut and bolt removed.
3 A simple continuity test and a short circuit test are the only checks that can be applied, usually with a bulb and a battery.

15 Courtesy light bulb: replacement - C70 model only

1 The courtesy light is mounted alongside the ignition switch, protruding through the left-hand cover.
2 To replace the bulb, remove the cover, rotate the plastic button and pull it clear to expose the bulb. The bulb rating is 3 watts.

16 Horn: location and adjustment

1 The horn is suspended from the air cleaner hose, underneath the legshields.
2 There is means of adjusting the horn note at the rear of the horn body. If the horn note is weak, the adjusting screw should be turned anticlockwise to increase the volume.

17 Ignition switch: general description

1 The ignition switch is operated by a key, which cannot be removed when the ignition is switched on.
2 The number stamped on the key will match the number on the lock. This will aid obtaining a replacement key, if the original is lost.
3 The ignition key operates also the steering head lock.
4 It is not practicable to repair the switch if it malfunctions. It should be replaced with another lock and key to match.

18 Lighting switch and indicator switch

1 The switches are mounted on the handlebars and are not

14.1 The resistance unit is mounted behind the steering head

15.1 The courtesy light is by the ignition switch

15.2 The cover unscrews to allow access to the bulb

16.1 The horn is mounted on the inlet air hose

repairable. If any are faulty or damaged they must be renewed as a complete unit.

2   On no account oil the switches or the oil will spread across the internal contacts and form an effective insulator.

19 Stop lamp switch: adjustment

1   The rear brake lever operated stop lamp switch is located forward of and above the right-hand swinging arm pivot point. The switch has a threaded body giving a range of adjustment and is retained in a frame-mounted bracket by an adjusting nut; a spring connects the switch to the brake pedal.

2   If the stop lamp is late in operating, hold the body of the switch and turn the adjusting nut so that the body moves away from the brake pedal. If the switch shows a tendency to stick on or operates too early, rotate the nut so the switch body moves towards the brake pedal. As a guide, the stop lamp should illuminate after the brake pedal has been depressed by about 20 mm (0.8 in) (measured at the pedal end).

20 Wiring: layout and inspection

1   The wiring harness is colour-coded and will correspond with the accompanying wiring diagrams.

2   Visual inspection will show whether any breaks or frayed outer coverings are giving rise to short circuits. Another source

19.2 Turn the nut to lower or raise the stop lamp switch body

of trouble may be the snap connectors, where the connector has not been pushed home fully in the outer housing.

3   Intermittent short circuits can often be traced to a chafed wire that passes through or close to a metal component, such as a frame member. Avoid tight bends in the wire or situations where the wire can become trapped between casings.

21 Fault diagnosis: electrical system

Symptom	Cause	Remedy
Complete electrical failure	Blown fuse	Locate fault and renew fuse.
	Broken wire from generator	Reconnect.
	Lighting switch faulty	Renew switch.
	Generator not charging	Check output.
Dim lights	Bad connections	Renovate, paying particular attention to earth connections.
Constantly 'blowing' bulbs	Vibration	Check bulb holders are secure.
	Poor earth connections	Renovate.
Indicators not working	Flat battery	Recharge battery and check generator output.
	Blown fuse	Check wiring before renewing 15 amp fuse.
	Isolated battery	Check battery connections. Clean any corrosion.
	Indicator switch faulty	Renew switch.

Fig. 7.1. Honda C50 Wiring Diagram

Fig. 7.2. Honda C70 Wiring Diagram

Fig. 7.3. Honda C90 Wiring Diagram

The Honda C50Z-A (C50L) model

The Honda C70Z-Z model

The Honda C90-E model

The Honda C90M-G model

Chapter 8 The 1977 on models

Contents

Specifications

Except where entered below, information for the later models is as specified in the preceding Chapters of this manual. For information on the C50Z-A (C50L) model, refer to that given for the C50Z-Z model. Information applies to all models unless otherwise stated.

Specifications relating to Chapter 1

Engine

Bore – C90-C, E, G, N, P, T, M-F, M-G, M-N, M-P, M-T . . .	47.0 mm (1.85 in)
Stroke – C90-C, E, G, N, P, T, M-F, M-G, M-N, M-P, M-T . .	49.5 mm (1.95 in)
Capacity – C90-C, E, G, N, P, T, M-F, M-G, M-N, M-P, M-T	85.8 cc (5.25 cu in)
Compression ratio:	
C50Z-Z, C50-C	9.5 : 1
C50-E	10.0 : 1
C70 – all models, C90-C, E, G, N, P, T, M-F, M-G, M-N,	
M-P, M-T	8.8 : 1

Connecting rod

Big-end maximum endfloat	0.6 mm (0.0236 in)
Big-end radial free play	0 – 0.012 mm (0 – 0.0005 in)
Service limit	0.05 mm (0.0020 in)
Small-end bore ID – C50/70Z-2 and Z-Z, C90-C, E, G, N,	
P, T, M-F, M-G, M-N, M-P, M-T	13.013 – 13.043 mm (0.5123 – 0.5135 in)
Service limit	13.100 mm (0.5157 in)
Small-end bore ID – C90Z-2, C90Z-Z	14.012 – 14.028 mm (0.5517 – 0.5523 in)
Service limit	14.050 mm (0.5532 in)
Crankshaft runout	0 – 0.015 mm (0 – 0.0006 in)
Service limit	0.100 mm (0.0039 in)

Piston

Skirt minimum OD	
C50Z-2, C50Z-Z	38.9 mm (1.5315 in)
C70Z-2 and Z-Z, C90-C, E, G, N, P, T, M-F, M-G, M -N,	
M-P, M-T	46.9 mm (1.8465 in)
C90Z-2, C90Z-Z	49.8 mm (1.9606 in)
Gudgeon pin OD:	
C50/70Z-2 and Z-Z, C90-C, E, G, N, P, T, M-F, M-G,	
M-N, M-P, M-T	12.994 – 13.000 mm (0.5116 – 0.5118 in)
Service limit	12.980 mm (0.5110 in)
C90Z-2, C90Z-Z	13.994 – 14.000 mm (0.5509 – 0.5512 in)
Service limit	13.960 mm (0.5496 in)

Compression ring end gap:
C50Z-2 and Z-Z, C90-C, E, G, N, P, T, M-F, M-G, M-N,
M-P, M-T . . . . 0.10 – 0.30 mm (0.0039 – 0.0118 in)
C70Z-2, C70Z-Z, C90Z-2, C90Z-Z . . . . 0.15 – 0.35 mm (0.0059 – 0.0138 in)
Service limit . . . . 0.50 mm (0.0196 in)
Compression ring/groove clearance:
All C50, C70 and C90Z-2 and Z-Z models . . . . . . 0.010 – 0.045 mm (0.0004 – 0.0018 in)
C90-C, E, G, N, P, T, M-F, M-G, M-N, M-P, M-T . . 0.015 – 0.050 mm (0.0006 – 0.0020 in)
Service limit . . . . 0.120 mm (0.0047 in)

Piston ring dimensions: . . . .

	C50Z-2, C50Z-Z	C70Z-2, C70Z-Z	C90Z-2, C90Z-Z
Top and second ring thickness	1.7 – 1.9 mm (0.0669 – 0.0748 in)	1.9 – 2.1 mm (0.748 – 0.0827 in)	1.175 – 1.190 mm (0.0463 – 0.0508 in)
Service limit	1.6 mm (0.0630 in)	1.8 mm (0.0709 in)	1.13 mm (0.0445 in)
Oil ring thickness	–	–	2.475 – 2.490 mm (0.0974 – 0.0980 in)
Service limit	–	–	2.43 mm (0.0956 in)
Top and second ring width	1.175 – 1.190 mm (0.0463 – 0.0469 in)	1.175 – 1.190 mm (0.0463 – 0.0469 in)	–
Service limit	1.12 mm (0.0441 in)	1.12 mm (0.0441 in)	-
Oil ring width	2.475 – 2.490 mm (0.0974 – 0.0980 in)	2.475 – 2.490 mm (0.0974 – 0.0980 in)	–
Service limit	2.42 mm (0.0953 in)	2.42 mm (0.0953 in)	–

Valves

Inlet valve stem minimum OD:
C50/70Z-2 and Z-Z, C90-C, E, G, N, P, T, M-F,
M-G, M-N, M-P, M-T . . . . 5.40 mm (0.2126 in)
C90Z-2, C90Z-Z . . . . 5.43 mm (0.2138 in)
Exhaust valve stem minimum OD:
C50/70Z-2 and Z-Z, C90-C, E, G, N, P, T, M-F,
M-G, M-N, M-P, M-T . . . . 5.40 mm (0.2126 in)
C90Z-2, C90Z-Z . . . . 5.41 mm (0.2130 in)
Valve stem/guide maximum clearance:
Inlet – all C50, C70 and C90Z-2 and Z-Z models . . 0.12 mm (0.0047 in)
Inlet – C70-C, E, C90-C, E, G, N, P, T, M-F, M-G,
M-N, M-P, M-T models . . . . 0.08 mm (0.0032 in)
Exhaust – except C50-C, C50-E . . . . 0.10 mm (0.0039 in)
Valve face width – except C50-C, C50-E . . . . 1.2 – 1.5 mm (0.0472 – 0.0591 in)
Service limit . . . . 1.8 mm (0.0709 in)
Valve spring free length:
Inner – C90Z-2, C90Z-Z . . . . 26.5 mm (1.0433 in)
Service limit . . . . 25.5 mm (1.0039 in)
Inner – all other models except C50-E . . . . 25.1 mm (0.9882 in)
Service limit . . . . 23.9 mm (0.9409 in)
Outer – C90Z-2, C90Z-Z . . . . 31.8 mm (1.2520 in)
Service limit . . . . 30.6 mm (1.2047 in)
Outer – all other models except C50-E . . . . 28.1 mm (1.1063 in)
Service limit . . . . 26.9 mm (1.0591 in)

Camshaft and rockers

	C50/70Z-2, Z-Z	C90Z-2, C90Z-Z	C90-C, E, G, N, P, T, M-F, M-G, M-N, M-P, M-T
Camshaft:			
Inlet lobe height	26.07 mm (1.0264 in)	24.90 – 24.98 mm (0.9803 – 0.9835 in)	27.945 mm (1.1002 in)
Service limit	25.69 mm (1.0114 in)	24.60 mm (0.9685 in)	27.55 mm (1.0846 in)
Exhaust lobe height	26.07 mm (1.0264 in)	24.90 – 24.98 mm (0.9803 – 0.9835 in)	26.076 mm (1.0266 in)
Service limit	25.69 mm (1.0114 in)	24.60 mm (0.9685 in)	25.69 mm (1.0114 in)
Journal diameter (right-hand end)	–	17.927 – 17.938 mm (0.7058 – 0.7062 in)	–
Service limit	–	17.90 mm (0.7047 in)	–
Journal diameter (left-hand end)	–	25.917 – 25.930 mm (1.0204 – 1.0209 in)	–
Service limit	–	25.80 mm (1.0157 in)	–
Bearing axial play	0.004 – 0.036 mm (0.0002 – 0.0014 in)	–	–
Service limit	0.1 mm (0.004 in)	–	–
Bearing radial play	0.010 – 0.025 mm (0.0004 – 0.0010 in)	–	0.010 – 0.025 mm (0.0004 – 0.0010 in)
Service limit	0.05 mm (0.002 in)	–	0.10 mm (0.004 in)
Bearing ID (right-hand end)	–	18.000 – 10.018 mm (0.7087 – 0.7094 in)	–
Service limit	–	18.05 mm (0.7106 in)	–
Bearing ID (left-hand end)	–	26.000 – 26.020 mm (1.0236 – 1.0244 in)	–
Service limit	–	26.05 mm (1.0256 in)	–

Rocker arm ID – C50, C70, C90Z-2 and Z-Z,
C90-C, E, G, N, P, T, M-F, M-G, M-N, M-P, M-T .. 10.000 – 10.015 mm (0.3937 – 0.3943 in)
Service limit . . . . 10.100 mm (0.3976 in)
Rocker shaft OD – C50/70Z-2 and Z-Z,
C90-C, E, G, N, P, T, M-F, M-G, M-N, M-P, M-T .. 9.978 – 9.987 mm (0.3928 – 0.3933 in)
Service limit . . . . 9.910 mm (0.3902 in)
Rocker shaft OD – C90Z-2, C90Z-Z . . . . 9.972 – 9.987 mm (0.3926 – 0.3932 in)
Service limit . . . . 9.920 mm (0.3906 in)

Gearbox

Reduction ratios:	C50Z-2, Z-Z, C	C50-E	C70- all models	C90Z-2, Z-Z	C90-C, E, G, N, P, T, M-F, M-G, M-N, M-P, M-T
1st	3.273:1 (36/11T)	3.181:1 (N/Av)	3.273:1 (36/11T)	2.538:1 (N/Av)	2.833:1 (34/12T)
2nd	1.823:1 (31/17T)	1.705:1 (N/Av)	1.722:1 (31/18T)	1.555:1 (N/Av)	1.647:1 (28/17T)
3rd	1.191:1 (25/12T)	1.238:1 (N/Av)	1.191:1 (25/12T)	1.000:1 (N/Av)	1.045:1 (23/22T)
4th	N/App	0.958:1 (N/Av)	N/App	N/App	N/App
Final drive	3.077:1 (40/13T)	3.231:1 142/13T)	2.571:1 (36/14T)	2.857:1 (40/14T)	2.600:1 (39/15T)

Selector drum OD:
C50/70Z-2, Z-Z, C90-C, E, G, N, P, T, M-F, M-G, M-N,
M-P, M-T . . . . 33.950 – 33.975 mm (1.3366 – 1.3376 in)
Service limit . . . . 33.930 mm (1.3358 in)
C90Z-2, Z-Z . . . . 41.950 – 41.975 mm (1.6516 – 1.6526 in)
Service limit . . . . 41.900 mm (1.6496 in)
Selector drum groove width . . . . 6.10 – 6.20 mm (0.2402 – 0.2441 in)
Service limit . . . . 6.30 mm (0.2480 in)
Selector fork ID:
C50/70Z-2, Z-Z . . . . 34.000 – 34.025 mm (1.3386 – 1.3396 in)
Service limit . . . . 34.065 mm (1.3411 in)
C90Z-2, Z-Z . . . . 42.000 – 42.025 mm (1.6535 – 1.6545 in)
Service limit . . . . 42.100 mm (1.6575 in)
Left-hand selector fork claw end thickness:
C50/70Z-2, Z-Z, C90-C, E, G, N, P, T, M-F, M-G, M-N,
M-P, M-T . . . . 4.860 – 4.940 mm (0.1913 – 0.1945 in)
Service limit . . . . 4.600 mm (0.1811 in)
C90Z-2, Z-Z . . . . 5.960 – 6.040 mm (0.2347 – 0.2378 in)
Service limit . . . . 5.850 mm (0.2303 in)
Right-hand selector fork claw end thickness:
C50/70Z-2, Z-Z, C90-C, E, G, N, P, T, M-F, M-G, M-N,
M-P, M-T . . . . 5.860 – 5.940 mm (0.2307 – 0.2339 in)
Service limit . . . . 5.600 mm (0.2205 in)
C90Z-2, Z-Z . . . . 5.960 – 6.040 mm (0.2347 – 0.2378 in)
Service limit . . . . 5.850 mm (0.2303 in)
Gearbox shaft OD – C90-C, E, G, N, P, T, M-F, M-G, M-N, M-P, M-T:
Mainshaft – at 2nd gear pinion . . . . 16.983 – 16.994 mm (0.6686 – 0.6691 in)
Service limit . . . . 16.950 mm (0.6673 in)
Layshaft – at 1st gear pinion . . . . 19.980 – 19.959 mm (0.7866 – 0.7858 in)
Service limit . . . . 19.940 mm (0.7850 in)
Layshaft – at 3rd gear pinion . . . . 16.466 – 16.484 mm (0.6483 – 0.6490 in)
Service limit . . . . 16.440 in (0.6472 in)
Gearbox shaft ID – C90-C, E, G, N, P, T, M-F, M-G, M-N, M-P, M-T:
Mainshaft – 2nd gear pinion . . . . 17.016 – 17.043 mm (0.6699 – 0.6710 in)
Service limit . . . . 17.100 mm (0.6732 in)
Layshaft – 1st gear pinion . . . . 20.020 – 20.053 mm (0.7882 – 0.7895 in)
Service limit . . . . 20.100 mm (0.7913 in)
Layshaft – 3rd gear pinion . . . . 16.516 – 16.543 mm (0.6502 – 0.6513 in)
Service limit . . . . 16.600 mm (0.6535 in)

Final drive chain

Size . . . . 420 (1/2 x 1/4 in)
Number of links:
All C50 models, C90-C, E, G, N, P, T, M-F, M-G,
M-N, M-P, M-T 98
All C70 models 96
C90Z-2, C90Z-Z 100

Specifications relating to Chapter 2

Clutch

Clutch spring free length:
C50Z-2, C50Z-Z, C50Z-A . . . . 22.55 mm (0.8878 in)
Service limit . . . . 20.65 mm (0.8130 in)

C70Z-2, C70Z-Z	25.08 mm (0.9874 in)
Service limit	23.08 mm (0.9087 in)
C90Z-2, C90Z-Z	23.40 mm (0.9213 in)
Service limit	22.00 mm (0.8661 in)
C90-C, C90-E	17.60 mm (0.6929 in)
Service limit	16.40 mm (0.6457 in)
C90-G, N, P, T, M-F, M-G, M-N, M-P, M-T	N/Av
Thickness of friction plate type A – internal splines:	
C50/70Z-2, Z-Z	2.55 – 2.65 mm (0.1004 – 0.1043 in)
Service limit	2.30 mm (0.0906 in)
C90Z-2, C90Z-Z	2.65 – 2.75 mm (0.1043 – 0.1083 in)
Service limit	2.40 mm (0.0945 in)
C50/70-C, E, C90-C, E, G, N, P, T, M-F, M-G,	
M-N, M-P, M-T	2.52 – 2.68 mm (0.0992 – 0.1055 in)
Service limit	2.30 mm (0.0906 in)
Thickness of friction plate type B – external tangs:	
All models except C90Z-2, Z-Z	3.35 – 3.45 mm (0.1319 – 0.1358 in)
Service limit	3.00 mm (0.1181 in)
Thickness of clutch plain plates:	
C90Z-2, C90Z-Z	1.95 – 2.05 mm (0.0768 – 0.0807 in)
Service limit	1.85 mm (0.0728 in)
Plain plate maximum warpage:	
C90Z-2, C90Z-Z	0.5 mm (0.0197 in)
All other models	0.2 mm (0.0079 in)
Primary driven gear ID:	
C90Z-2, C90Z-Z	24.000 – 24.020 mm (0.9449 – 0.9457 in)
Service limit	24.150 mm (0.9508 in)
C50/70-C, E, C90-C, E, G, N, P, T, M-F, M-G,	
M-N, M-P, M-T	21.000 – 21.021 mm (0.8268 – 0.8276 in)
Service limit	21.050 mm (0.8287 in)
Centre guide/bush OD:	
C90Z-2, C90Z-Z	23.935 – 23.955 mm (0.9423 – 0.9431 in)
Service limit	23.850 mm (0.9390 in)
C50/70-C, E, C90-C, E, G, N, P, T, M-F, M-G,	
M-N, M-P, M-T	20.930 – 20.950 mm (0.8240 – 0.8248 in)
Service limit	20.900 mm (0.8228 in)

Specifications relating to Chapter 3

Fuel tank capacity

Overall – all C50/70/90-C, E models	4.0 lit (7.04 pint)
Overall – C90-G, N, P, T, M-F, M-G, M-N, M-P, M-T .	3.5 lit (6.16 pint)
Reserve – C90Z-2, C90Z-Z	1.0 lit (1.76 pint)
Reserve – C50/70Z-2, Z-Z, C50Z-A, C50/70/90-C .	0.8 lit (1.41 pint)

Carburettor	**C50Z-2**	**C50Z-Z**	**C50Z-A**	**C50-C**	**C50-E**
ID number	PB40A-C	PB40B-A	PB40B-B	PB46A-B	PB79A-A
Main jet	68	78	78	70	N/Av
Pilot jet	35	35	35	38	N/Av
Pilot mixture screw – turns out fully in	1 7/8	2 1/2	2 1/2	1 1/2	1 7/8
Float height	10 mm (0.394 in)	10.7 mm (0.421 in)	10.7 mm (0.421 in)	N/Av	N/Av
Needle clip position – grooves from top	3rd	2nd	2nd	N/Av	N/Av
Idle speed (rpm)	1500 ± 100	1500 ± 100	1500 ± 100	1700	1700

Carburettor	**C70Z-2**	**C70Z-Z**	**C70-C**	**C70-E**	**C90Z-2**
ID number	PB35A-C	PB35B-A	PB47A-B	N/Av	PB25A-A/B
Main jet	72	75	78	78	78
Pilot jet	35	35	38	38	38
Pilot mixture screw – turns out fully in	1 1/2	2	1 3/4	1 7/8	1 1/8
Float height	10.0 mm (0.394 in)	10.7 mm (0.421 in)	N/Av	N/Av	10.0 mm (0.394 in)
Needle clip position – grooves from top	3rd	3rd	N/Av	N/Av	3rd
Idle speed (rpm)	1500 ± 100	1500 ± 100	1700	1700	1400

Carburettor	**C90Z-Z**	**C90-C**	**C90-E, G, N, P, T, M-F, M-G, M-N, M-P, M-T**
ID number	PB25A-B	PB48A-B	PB81A-A/F (C90-E, G, N, M-F, M-G, M-N), PB58E-A/B (C90-P, T, M-P, M-T)
Main jet	78	80	85
Pilot jet	38	40	40
Pilot mixture screw – turns out fully in	1 1/8	1 3/8	1 3/4
Float height	10 mm (0.394 in)	10.7 mm (0.421 in)	10.7 mm (0.421 in)
Needle clip position – grooves from top	3rd	3rd	3rd
Idle speed (rpm)	1400	1700	1700

Oil pump

Outer rotor/pump body clearance service limit . . . . 0.2 mm (0.0079 in)
Inner and outer rotor end clearance service limit . . . 0.12 mm (0.0047 in)

Oil capacity – C50/70-C, E, C90-C, E, G, N, P, T, M-F, M-G, M-N, M-P, M-T

At oil change . . . . 0.6 lit (1.06 pint)
At engine rebuild . . . . 0.8 lit (1.41 pint)
Recommended oil . . . . SAE 10W40 SE or SF

Specifications relating to Chapter 4

Generator output

C50/70Z-2 . . . . 0.041 kW @ 8000 rpm
C50/70Z-Z . . . . 0.064 kW @ 5000 rpm

Spark plug

	NGK	ND
Make		
Type:		
C90Z-2, C90Z-Z	DR6HS	X20FSR-U
C50-E	CR6HS	U20FSR-U
All other models	CR7HS	U22FSR-U

Condenser – Z-2, Z-Z models only

Capacity . . . . 0.27 – 0.33 microfarad

Ignition system

Type – C50/70-C, E, C90-C, E, G, N, P, T, M-F, M-G, M-N,
M-P, M-T . . . . CDI (Capacitor Discharge Ignition)

Specifications relating to Chapter 5

Front suspension

Spring free length:
  C50/70Z-2, Z-Z . . . . 130.7 mm (5.1457 in)
  Service limit . . . . 122.0 mm (4.8031 in)
  C90Z-2, Z-Z . . . . 133.4 mm (5.2520 in)
  Service limit . . . . 120.0 mm (4.7244 in)
Leading link pivot bearing:
  Outer bush ID . . . . 14.000 – 14.100 mm (0.5512 – 0.5551 in)
  Service limit . . . . 14.470 mm (0.5697 in)
  Inner spacer OD . . . . 13.960 – 13.980 mm (0.5496 – 0.5504 in)
  Service limit . . . . 13.550 mm (0.5335 in)
Suspension unit bottom mounting:
  Outer bush ID . . . . 12.000 – 12.100 mm (0.4724 – 0.4764 in)
  Service limit . . . . 12.410 mm (0.4886 in)
  Inner spacer OD . . . . 11.960 – 11.980 mm (0.4709 – 0.4717 in)
  Service limit . . . . 11.610 mm (0.4571 in)

Rear suspension

Spring free length:
  C50/70Z-2 . . . . 209.9 mm (8.2638 in)
  Service limit . . . . 198.7 mm (7.8228 in)
  C50/70Z-Z . . . . 215.6 mm (8.4882 in)
  Service limit . . . . 206.4 mm (8.1260 in)
  C90Z-2, Z-Z . . . . 212.0 mm (8.3464 in)
  Service limit . . . . 209.0 mm (8.2283 in)
  C50/70/90-C . . . . 219.3 mm (8.6338 in)
  Service limit . . . . 215.0 mm (8.4646 in)
  C50/70-E, C90-E, G, N, P, T, M-F, M-G, M-N,
    M-P, M-T . . . . 219.6 mm (8.6457 in)
  Service limit . . . . 215.0 mm (8.4646 in)

Specifications relating to Chapter 6

Wheels

Rim size – front and rear . . . . 1.40 x 17
Rim maximum runout – radial and axial . . . . 2.0 mm (0.0787 in)
Spindle maximum warpage . . . . 0.2 mm (0.0079 in)

Brakes – front and rear

Friction material thickness . . . . 3.9 – 4.0 mm (0.1535 – 0.1575 in)
Service limit . . . . 2.0 mm (0.0787 in)
Drum ID . . . . 109.8 – 110.2 mm (4.3228 – 4.3386 in)
Service limit . . . . 111.0 mm (4.370 in)

Tyres

Rear tyre size – C50-C, E, all C70 models	2.50 x 17
Tyre pressures – tyres cold:	
Front:	
C50/70/90Z-2, Z-Z	25 psi (1.75 kg/cm²)
C50/70-C, E, C90-C, E, G, N, P, T, M-F, M-G, M-N, M-P, M-T	28 psi (2.00 kg/cm²)
Rear – with pillion passenger:	
C50/70-C, E, C90-C, E, G, N, P, T, M-F, M-G, M-N, M-P, M-T	40 psi (2.80 kg/cm²)

Specifications relating to Chapter 7

Electrical system

Voltage:	
C50/70/90Z-2, Z-Z	6
C50/70-C, E, C90-C, E, G, N, P, T, M-F, M-G, M-N, M-P, M-T	12

Battery capacity

C90Z-2, Z-Z	5.5 Ah
C50/70-C, E, C90-C, E, G, N, P, T	4 Ah (Yuasa 12N4/YB4L-B)
C90M-F, M-G, M-N, M-P, M-T	5 Ah (Yuasa YB5L-B)

Fuse rating

C50/70/90-C	10 amp
C50/70-E, C90-E, G, N, P, T, M-F, M-G, M-N, M-P, M-T	7 amp

Bulbs

	C50/70/90Z-2, Z-Z	C50/70/90-C	C50/70-E, C90-E, M-F	C90-G, N, P, T, M-G, M-F, M-N, M-P, M-T
Headlamp	6V, 25/25W	12V, 25/25W	12V, 25/25W	12V, 25/25W
Pilot lamp	6V, 5W	12V, 4W	12V, 4W	12V, 4W
Stop/tail lamp	6V, 21/5W	12V, 21/5W	12V, 21/5W	12V, 21/5W
Flashing indicator lamps	6V, 18W	12V, 18W	12V, 18W	12V, 10W
Speedometer illuminating lamp(s)	6V, 1.5W	12V, 2W	12V, 1.7W (x2)	12V, 1.7W (x2)
Neutral and flashing indicator warning lamps	6V, 1.7W	12V, 3.4W	12V, 3.4W	12V 3.4W
Main beam warning lamp	N/App	N/App	N/App	12V 1.7W

Torque wrench settings

Component	kgf m	lbf ft
Cylinder head nuts:		
C50/70Z-2, Z-Z, C90-C, E, G, N, P, T, M-F, M-G, M-N, M-P, M-T	0.9 – 1,2	6.5 – 9
C90Z-2, Z-Z	2.0 – 2.5	14.5 – 18
Camshaft sprocket bolts:		
C50/70Z-2, Z-Z	0.5 – 0.9	3.5 – 6.5
C90Z-2, Z-Z	0.9 – 1.2	6.5 – 9
C90-C, E, G, N, P, T, M-F, M-G, M-N, M-P, M-T . .	0.7 – 1.1	5 – 8
Camchain guide roller bolt – C50/70/90Z-2, Z-Z . . .	0.9 – 1.4	6.5 – 10
Camchain tensioner sealing plug – C90-C, E, G, N, P, T, M-F, M-G, M-N, M-P, M-T	2.0 – 2.5	14.5 – 18
Clutch centre nut – except C50/70-C, E	3.8 – 4.5	27.5 – 32.5
Flywheel generator rotor nut/bolt:		
C50/70Z-2, Z-Z	2.4 – 3.0	17 – 22
C90Z-2, Z-Z	2.6 – 3.2	19 – 23
C90-C, E, G, N, P, T, M-F, M-G, M-N, M-P, M-T . .	3.0 – 3.8	22 – 27.5
Flywheel generator stator bolts – C90Z-2, Z-Z	0.8 – 1.2	6 – 9
Crankcase and crankcase cover screws except C50/70-C, E	0.7 – 1.1	5 – 8
Selector drum retaining bolt – C90Z-2, Z-Z	0.8 – 1.2	6 – 9
Selector drum index arm pivot bolt:		
C50/70/90Z-2, Z-Z	0.8 – 1.2	6 – 9
C90-C, E, G, N, P, T, M-F, M-G, M-N, M-P, M-T . .	0.9 – 1.4	6.5 – 10
Gearchange and kickstart lever pinch bolts	0.8 – 1.2	6 – 9
Engine oil drain plug	2.0 – 2.5	14.5 – 18
Automatic advance unit centre bolt – C90Z-2, Z-Z .	0.8 – 1.2	6 – 9
Fuel tap filter bowl – C50/70-C, E, C90-C, E, G, N, P, T, M-F, M-G, M-N, M-P, M-T	0.3 – 0.5	2 – 3.5
Steering stem nut:		
C50/70/90Z-2, Z-Z	6.0 – 8.0	43 – 58
C90-C, E, G, N, P, T, M-F, M-G, M-N, M-P, M-T . .	6.0 – 9.0	43 – 65
Handlebar mounting nuts or bolts:		
C50/70/90Z-2, Z-Z	2.0 – 2.5	14.5 – 18
C90-C, E, G, N, P, T, M-F, M-G, M-N, M-P, M-T . .	2.0 – 3.0	14.5 – 22

Front suspension arm pivot bolt:		
C50/70Z-2, Z-Z	2.0 – 2.5	14.5 – 18
C90Z-2, Z-Z	2.0 – 3.5	14.5 – 25
C90-C, E, G, N, P, T, M-F, M-G, M-N, M-P, M-T	2.0 – 3.0	14.5 – 22
Front suspension unit mounting bolt:		
C50/70Z-2, Z-Z	1.5 – 2.0	11 – 14.5
C90Z-2, Z-Z	2.0 – 3.5	14.5 – 25
C90-C, E, G, N, P, T, M-F, M-G, M-N, M-P, M-T	2.0 – 2.5	14.5 – 18
Rear suspension unit mounting nuts or bolts –		
except C50/70-C, E	2.5 – 3.5	18 – 25
Swinging arm pivot bolt:		
C50/70Z-2, Z-Z, C90-C, E, G, N, P, T, M-F, M-G,		
M-N, M-P, M-T	2.5 – 3.5	18 – 25
C90Z-2, Z-Z	3.0 – 4.0	22 – 29
Engine mounting bolts:		
C50/70Z-2, Z-Z, C90-C, E, G, N, P, T, M-F, M-G,		
M-N, M-P, M-T	2.0 – 2.5	14.5 – 18
C90Z-2, Z-Z	3.0 – 4.0	22 – 29
Front wheel spindle nut:		
C50/70Z-2, Z-Z	4.0 – 5.0	29 – 36
C90Z-2, Z-Z	3.5 – 5.0	25 – 36
C50/70-C, E, C90-C, E, G, N, M-F, M-G, M-N	3.0 – 4.0	22 – 29
C90-P, T, M-P, M-T	N/Av	
Rear wheel spindle nut:		
C90-P, T, M-P, M-T	N/Av	
Except C90Z-2, Z-Z	4.0 – 5.0	29 – 36
C90Z-2, Z-Z	3.5 – 5.0	25 – 36
Rear wheel spindle sleeve nut	3.5 – 4.5	25 – 32.5
Rear brake torque arm nuts:		
C50/70Z-2, Z-Z	1.0 – 2.0	7 – 14.5
C90Z-2, Z-Z	2.0 – 2.5	14.5 – 18
C50/70-C, E, C90-C, E, G, N, P, T, M-F, M-G,		
M-N, M-P, M-T	1.8 – 2.5	13 – 18
Rear wheel sprocket nuts:		
C50/70Z-2, Z-Z	1.8 – 2.3	13 – 16.5
C90Z-2, Z-Z	1.8 – 2.5	13 – 18
C90-C, E, G, N, P, T, M-F, M-G, M-N, M-P, M-T	2.7 – 3.0	19.5 – 22

1 Introduction

The first seven Chapters of this manual cover the C50, C70 and C90 models sold in the UK up to July 1977; this Chapter refers to all subsequent variations of those models sold since, giving information on specifications and workshop procedures only where this is significantly different from that given in the preceding Chapters. When working on a later model always refer to this Chapter first; where no information is given it can be assumed that the procedure is essentially the same as that described for the earlier models.

It is essential to identify exactly the model being worked on; to assist the owner in this, the major identifying points of each are given below with the relevant frame numbers, where available. Where only one frame number is given, this is the number at which that particular model's production run commenced. Note that it is not sufficient to identify a machine by its date of registration (or sale); while this date will usually correspond with the dates of import given on page 1 of this Manual, this may not always be the case. The frame number is the only accurate means of identifying a particular model.

The Z-2 models are largely identical to the original versions, the only significant difference being the fitting of a new type of carburettor with a handlebar-mounted choke operated by cable. The Z-Z models can be identified by the conical-ended silencer. They employed modified components to give a revised gear selection pattern. The C50Z-A model, usually known as the C50L, was fitted with a single seat and carrier, but in all other respects it is the same as the C50Z-Z; to comply with the new legal definition of a moped it had no provision for carrying a pillion passenger. **Note:** *The C50L must not be confused with the later C50LA models which employ a 3-speed fully automatic transmission and are not covered in this Manual.*

The C50-C, C70-C and C90-C models are easily distinguished by their two-tone dualseats and restyled headlamp cowling and legshields. They all feature modified air filters, 12 volt electrics and CDI ignition systems. In addition to this, the C90 engine/gearbox unit was completely redesigned and is now exactly the same in layout as that of the C70 model, its new bore and stroke dimensions giving a capacity of 86 cc.

The C70-E and C90-E models, also known as the 'Super Cub' or 'Economy' models, are largely the same as the -C models but feature heavily revised cycle parts with more angular styling and are fitted with larger, rectangular flashing indicator lamps and headlamps; a fuel gauge is fitted and the handlebar controls improved. The C90-E is fitted with modified selector components which enable neutral to be selected in one movement when the machine is stationary. The C50-E received the same styling alterations and new features described above but was also fitted with a completely redesigned engine/gearbox unit which featured many modifications to improve fuel economy; amongst other new features, a 4-speed transmission is employed.

The C90-G, N, P and T models differ only in minor detail from the C90-E, and can be distinguished by their matt black-finished indicator lamps.

The C90-M models are fitted with an electric start, the motor being bolted to a modified left-hand engine cover and driving the crankshaft via a chain and a roller-type clutch mounted on the inner face of the (reversed) generator rotor. The generator coils are now mounted on the inside of the left-hand engine cover; apart from minor alterations which do not affect servicing procedures the engine is otherwise exactly the same as the standard, kickstart-only, models. The electrical system incorporates a larger-capacity battery as well as the starter button and relay. The cycle parts remain unchanged. The earlier C90M-F model can be distinguished only by its chrome-plated flashing indicator lamps as opposed to the matt black-finished lamps fitted to the later C90M-G, M-N, M-P and M-T models; apart from this the differences are minor.

The frame numbers by which each model can be identified are as follows:

Model	Frame number
C50Z-2	C50-5265598 to C50-5449865
C50Z-Z	C50Z-6000027
C50Z-A (C50L)	C50-7000001
C50-C	C50-8170046
C50-E	N/Av
C70Z-2	C70-6115364 to C70-6193904
C70Z-Z	C70Z-7000026
C70-C	C70-8022434 to C70-8039828
C70-E	N/Av
C90Z-2	C90-5104865 to C90-5132699
C90Z-Z	C90-5133011
C90-C	HA02-1122937 to HA02-1129446
C90-E	HA02-1335426
C90-G	HA02-1392669 to HA02-1460128
C90-N	HA02-5200001
C90-P	HA02-5300028
C90-T	HA02B*TK000001
C90M-F	HA02-1364806 to 1395407
C90M-G	HA02-1395328 to 1459318
C90M-N	HA02-5200001
C90M-P	HA02-5300035
C90M-T	HA02A*TK000001

2 Modifications to the engine/gearbox unit: general

1 On C90-C, E, G, N, P, T, M-F, M-G, M-N, M-P, M-T models the engine/gearbox is now of similar design and construction to that of the C50/70 models described in Chapter 1. Refer to the instructions given for those models when working on these later C90 machines.

2 On C70-E models, note that the outer valve springs are now fitted with bottom seats as shown for the C90 models in Fig. 1.5 of Chapter 1.

3 On all later models, when working on any part of the gearbox or the gear selector mechanism, note that several modifications have been made to these components. Refer to the appropriate illustration accompanying this text to ensure that all components are refitted in their correct positions.

4 The electric starter system fitted to C90M models is described in the relevant Sections at the end of this Chapter. Apart from the starter motor and drive, and the modified generator and left-hand engine cover, the remainder of the engine/transmission unit is essentially similar to the C50/70 unit described in Chapter 1.

1 Mainshaft
2 Mainshaft left-hand bearing
3 Mainshaft 2nd gear pinion
4 Splined thrust washer – 2 off
5 Circlip – 2 off
6 Mainshaft 3rd gear pinion
7 Thrust washer
8 Layshaft
9 Layshaft left-hand bearing
10 Oil seal
11 Sprocket
12 Lock washer
13 Bolt – 2 off
14 Layshaft 3rd gear pinion
15 Layshaft 2nd gear pinion
16 Layshaft 1st gear pinion
17 Thrust washer
18 Return spring
19 Kickstart spindle
20 Oil seal
21 Ratchet spring

Fig. 8.1 Gearbox components and kickstart spindle assembly – C90Z-Z models

Fig. 8.2 Gearbox components – C70-C, E and C50-C

1 Mainshaft
2 Thrust washer
3 Mainshaft 2nd gear pinion
4 Splined thrust washer – 2 off
5 Circlip – 4 off
6 Mainshaft 3rd gear pinion
7 Washer – C50 only
8 Mainshaft right-hand bearing
9 Layshaft
10 Layshaft left-hand bearing
11 Oil seal
12 Sprocket
13 Lock washer
14 Bolt – 2 off
15 Thrust washer
16 Layshaft 1st gear pinion
17 Splined thrust washer .
18 Layshaft 2nd gear pinion
19 Layshaft 3rd gear pinion
20 Bush – C70 only

Fig. 8.3 Gearbox components – C50-E model

1 Mainshaft
2 Mainshaft left-hand bearing
3 Mainshaft 2nd gear pinion
4 Splined thrust washer – 2 off
5 Circlip – 2 off
6 Mainshaft 3rd gear pinion
7 Mainshaft 4th gear pinion
8 Mainshaft right-hand bearing
9 Layshaft
10 Layshaft left-hand bearing
11 Oil seal
12 Sprocket
13 Lock washer
14 Bolt – 2 off
15 Thrust washer
16 Layshaft 1st gear pinion
17 Bush
18 Splined thrust washer
19 Circlip – 2 off
20 Layshaft 2nd gear pinion
21 Splined thrust washer – 2 off
22 Layshaft 3rd gear pinion
23 Layshaft 4th gear pinion
24 Layshaft right-hand bearing
25 Spring clip
26 Washer
27 Plate

Fig. 8.4 Gearbox components – C90-C, E, G, N, P, T, M-F, M-G, M-N, M-P, M-T models

1 Mainshaft
2 Thrust washer
3 Mainshaft 2nd gear pinion
4 Splined thrust washer
5 Circlip – 2 off
6 Mainshaft 3rd gear pinion
7 Mainshaft right-hand bearing
8 Layshaft
9 Thrust washer
10 Layshaft left-hand bearing
11 Oil seal
12 Sprocket
13 Lock washer
14 Bolt – 2 off
15 Layshaft 1st gear pinion
16 Splined thrust washer
17 Circlip
18 Layshaft 2nd gear pinion
19 Layshaft 3rd gear pinion
20 Bush
21 Spring clip*
22 Plate*
23 Washer
*All models except C90-C

Fig. 8.5 Gear selector mechanism – C90Z-2 and Z-Z models

1	Gearchange shaft	7	Screw	13	Neutral switch contact	18	Selector fork pin – 2 off
2	Return spring	8	Index plate	14	Washer	19	Pin clip – 2 off
3	Oil seal	9	Index pin – 2 off	15	Bolt	20	Index arm
4	Spring anchor	10	Index pin – 2 off	16	Selector fork	21	Return spring
5	Gearchange arm	11	Index pin	17	Selector fork	22	Index arm pivot bolt
6	Spring	12	Gearchange drum				

Fig. 8.6 Gear selector mechanism – C50/70-C, E models and C90-C, E, G, N, P, T, M-F, M-G, M-N, M-P, M-T models

1	Gearchange shaft	8	Index plate	15	Selector fork pin – 2 off	22	Index arm pivot bolt
2	Return spring	9	Roller – 2 off	16	Pin clip – 2 off	23	Return spring
3	Oil seal	10	Index pin – 4 off	17	Neutral switch contact	24	O-ring
4	Spring anchor	11	Index pin – C50E only	18	Washer	25	Neutral indicator switch
5	Gearchange arm	12	Selector fork	19	Bolt	26	Retaining plate
6	Spring	13	Selector fork	20	Plug	27	Screw
7	Bolt	14	Gearchange drum	21	Index arm		

Fig. 8.7 Kickstart assembly – C50/70-C, E models and C90-C, E, G, N, P, T, M-F, M-G, M-N, M-P, M-T models

1	*Kickstart spindle*	3	*Thrust washer*	5	*Kickstart ratchet*	7	*Washer*	9 *Spring inner*
2	*Kickstart pinion*	4	*Circlip*	6	*Ratchet spring*	8	*Return spring*	10 *Circlip*

3   Cam chain tensioner: general

C50/C70, Z-2 and Z-Z models

1 These models are fitted with the manual type of tensioner shown in Fig. 1.14, the tensioner having two springs and a slotted adjusting screw; it must be checked at regular intervals and reset manually as described in Routine Maintenance.

C90Z-2 and Z-Z models

2 These models are fitted with the manual type of tensioner shown in Fig. 1.13, the tensioner having the adjusting screw assembly (item 8). The tensioner must be checked at regular intervals and reset manually at the adjusting screw set in the sealing plug on the crankcase underside, as described in Routine Maintenance.

C50/70-C, E models and C90-C, E, G, N, P, T, M-F, M-G, M-N, M-P, M-T models

3 These models are fitted with an hydraulically operated tensioner that is completely automatic and requires no regular adjustment. Refer to the illustration accompanying this text for details.
4 To dismantle the tensioner, drain the engine oil and remove the generator components as described in Chapter 1, then unscrew the bolt and sealing washer from just in front of the gearchange shaft and the sealing plug from the crankcase underside. Withdraw the tensioner spring and pushrod.
5 Renew the spring if its overall free length (including cap) has settled to a length of 77 mm (3.0315 in) or less; a new spring should be 82.8 mm (3.2598 in) long. Wash the pushrod in solvent to remove all traces of oil and dirt. If the ball valve is jammed, if the pushrod is scratched or scored or if its body has worn at any point to an outside diameter of 11.94 mm (0.4701 in) or less, it must be renewed; a new pushrod should measure 11.985 – 12.000 mm (0.4719 – 0.4724 in). Check that the crankcase passage and oilways are completely clean and unworn; all other tensioner components are checked as described in Chapter 1.

6 On reassembly, oil thoroughly the pushrod before refitting it then insert the tensioner spring; refer to the illustration to ensure that both these components are refitted the correct way; note that the spring's smaller coils (and cap) must be uppermost. Fit the sealing plug and its washer tightening the plug to a torque setting of 2.0 – 2.5 kgf m (14.5 – 18 lbf ft). Inject 1 cc of oil into the crankcase passage before refitting the bolt and its sealing washer.

4   Clutch: general – C50/70-C, E models and C90-C, E, G, N, P, T, M-F, M-G, M-N, M-P, M-T models

Refer to the illustration accompanying this text when working on the clutch which is altered only slightly to combine the design of two types described in Chapter 2.

3.4 Remove sealing plug and bolt (arrowed) to release tensioner components – C50/70-C, E models and C90-C, E, G, N, P, T, M-F, M-G, M-N, M-P, M-T models

Fig. 8.8 Cam chain and tensioner – C50/70-C, E models and C90-C, E, G, N, P, T, M-F, M-G, M-N, M-P, M-T models

1	Cam chain	5	Bolt	9	Spindle	13	Pushrod	17	Sealing washer
2	Camshaft sprocket	6	Washer	10	Pivot bolt	14	Pushrod head	18	Sealing plug
3	Plate	7	Guide roller	11	Tensioner sprocket	15	Tensioner spring	19	Sealing washer
4	Bolt – 3 off	8	Guide sprocket	12	Tensioner arm	16	Bolt		

5 Carburettor: removal and refitting

1 Proceed as described in Section 7 of Chapter 3, noting the following additional points. The carburettor top should be unscrewed first and the throttle valve (slide) assembly withdrawn to provide working space; take care not to bend or damage the needle. Disconnect the choke cable by slackening the single clamp screw and disengage the cable end nipple from the operating arm.

2 On disconnecting the fuel feed pipes, the tank can be drained first, if required, but a simpler alternative is to pull each pipe off its stub on the tap assembly and plug it, using a screw or bolt of suitable size. To identify the main and reserve feed pipes, use screws or bolts that are markedly different in appearance and make a note before disconnecting them. Unscrew the two mounting bolts to release the carburettor.

3 On refitting, be careful to ensure that the main and reserve (where fitted) fuel feed pipes are refitted to their correct stubs, and secure them with the wire clips. Check that the insulator and sealing O-rings are correctly positioned before tightening the carburettor mounting bolts. On refitting the throttle valve assembly, take care not to bend or damage the needle, which should enter smoothly into the needle jet; check also that the throttle valve is aligned correctly with its cutaway towards the air filter. A locating pin set in the carburettor body should engage with the slot in the valve.

4 Engage the choke cable end nipple in the operating arm and place the cable outer between the two halves of its clamp. Check that the control knob is pushed fully in and pull the cable outer gently upwards until there is only very slight free play in the cable, then tighten the clamp screw. Operate the control knob several times, checking that the operating arm

moves smoothly and easily throughout its full range and that it returns fully to the off position when the knob is pushed in.

5 Carburettor adjustment is described in Section 7 of this Chapter.

6 Carburettor: dismantling, examination and reassembly

1 Referring to the illustrations accompanying this text, proceed as described in Sections 8, 9 and 10 of Chapter 3, noting the following points.

2 To remove the tap unit from the float chamber, remove its two retaining screws and withdraw the unit, followed by its sealing O-ring. On all Z-2 and Z-Z models the filter gauze can now be displaced for cleaning; on all later models the filter bowl must be unscrewed from the base of the tap unit and its sealing O-ring withdrawn before the filter gauze can be removed with its sealing O-ring.

3 Use only a fine-bristled toothbrush or similar to clean the filter gauze but note that the gauze must be renewed if it is split or damaged. The tap unit cannot be dismantled further and must be renewed as a complete assembly if it is leaking or damaged.

4 Unscrew its two retaining screws to release the float chamber, noting the sealing O-ring, then remove the float pivot pin and withdraw the float assembly and needle valve. Renew the floats if they are leaking or damaged. The float needle should be renewed if a wear ridge can be detected on its tip.

5 Use only a close-fitting spanner or screwdriver to unscrew the carburettor jets, but note that on some models the pilot jet is pressed into place and cannot be removed; in such cases extreme care must be taken to ensure that the jet is completely clear before the carburettor is reassembled. The needle jet is

Fig. 8.9 Clutch – C50/70-C, E models and C90-C, E, G, N, P, T, M-F, M-G, M-N, M-P, M-T models

1 Bearing
2 Screw – 4 off
3 Outer cover
4 Gasket
5 Nut
6 Lock washer

7 Tab washer
8 Clutch drum
9 Damper spring – 4 off
10 Screw – 4 off
11 Washer – 4 off
12 Clutch spring – 4 off

13 Circlip
14 Drive plate
15 Bob-weight clip
16 Bob-weight clip – 16 off C50,
   28 off C70/90
17 Clutch centre

18 Drive gear outer
19 Clutch plate
20 Clutch plate spring – 4 off
21 Friction plate A
22 Friction plate B
23 Clutch plate

24 Circlip
25 Primary driven gear
26 Bush
27 Spacer
28 Primary drive gear
29 Circlip

FWD

5.1a Unscrew carburettor top and withdraw throttle valve (slide) assembly

5.1b Slacken screw clamping choke outer cable ...

5.1c ... and push operating arm up so that nipple can be removed

5.2a Be careful to mark fuel pipes before disconnecting so that they can be refitted correctly (early models)

5.2b Disconnect all drain and breather hoses ...

5.2c ... slacken screw clamp and withdraw air filter hose ...

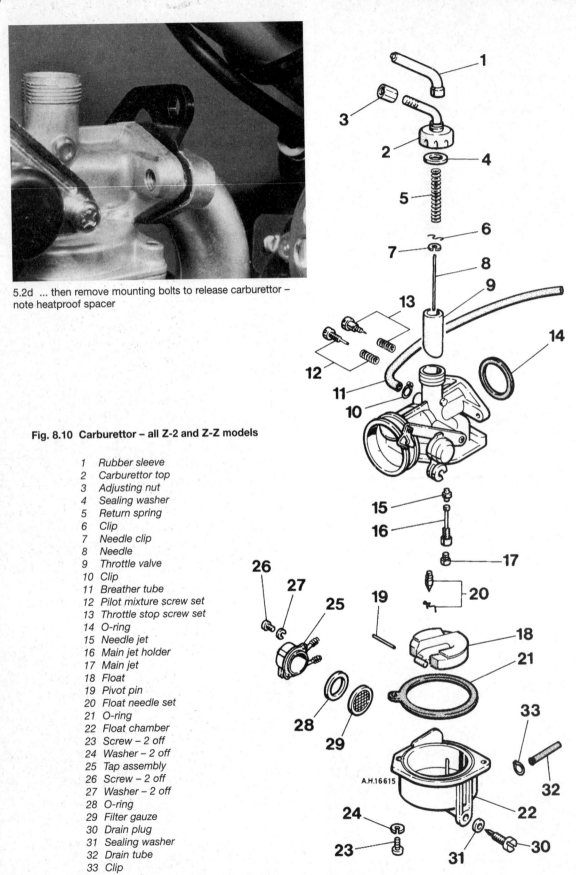

5.2d ... then remove mounting bolts to release carburettor – note heatproof spacer

Fig. 8.10 Carburettor – all Z-2 and Z-Z models

1   Rubber sleeve
2   Carburettor top
3   Adjusting nut
4   Sealing washer
5   Return spring
6   Clip
7   Needle clip
8   Needle
9   Throttle valve
10 Clip
11 Breather tube
12 Pilot mixture screw set
13 Throttle stop screw set
14 O-ring
15 Needle jet
16 Main jet holder
17 Main jet
18 Float
19 Pivot pin
20 Float needle set
21 O-ring
22 Float chamber
23 Screw – 2 off
24 Washer – 2 off
25 Tap assembly
26 Screw – 2 off
27 Washer – 2 off
28 O-ring
29 Filter gauze
30 Drain plug
31 Sealing washer
32 Drain tube
33 Clip

A.H.16615

Fig. 8.11 Carburettor – C50/70-C, E models and C90-C, E, G, N, P, T, M-F, M-G, M-N, M-P, M-T models

1 Rubber sleeve
2 Carburettor top
3 Adjusting nut
4 Sealing washer
5 Return spring
6 Clip
7 Needle clip
8 Needle
9 Throttle valve
10 Clip
11 Breather tube
12 Pilot mixture screw set
13 Throttle stop screw set
14 O-ring
15 Needle jet
16 Main jet holder
17 Main jet
18 Pilot jet
19 Float
20 Pivot pin
21 Float needle
22 O-ring
23 Float chamber
24 O-ring
25 Filter gauze
26 O-ring
27 Filter bowl
28 Screw – 2 off
29 O-ring
30 Tap assembly
31 Washer – 2 off
32 Screw – 2 off
33 O-ring
34 Drain plug
35 Drain tube
36 Circlip

6.2a Fuel tap assembly is retained by two screws

6.2b Filter gauze is behind tap on Z-2 and Z-Z models – note sealing O-ring

6.2c Removing filter gauze – later models – unscrew filter bowl ...

6.2d ... withdraw large sealing O-ring ...

6.2e ... and pull out filter gauze – note small O-ring

6.4a Remove two screws to release float chamber ...

6.4b ... then extract float pivot pin and withdraw float assembly

6.4c Renew float needle if its tip is worn or ridged

6.5a Main jet is screwed into jet holder – note that pilot jet cannot be removed on carburettor shown

6.5b Unscrew jet holder to release needle jet ...

6.5c ... which is pressed out from above

6.6 Check choke components carefully – carburettor must be renewed if wear is found

6.7a Proceed as described in text to remove and refit pilot mixture screw ...

6.7b ... and throttle stop screw

6.11 Ensure float engages correctly with needle on fitting

11 On reassembly, be careful not to overtighten the jets or component retaining screws; the jets and carburettor castings are delicate and can be easily damaged if mishandled.

7   Carburettor: settings and adjustment

1 The method of adjusting the type of carburettor fitted to the above listed models is similar to that given in Section 11 of Chapter 3. Note the pilot mixture screw settings listed in the Specifications Section of this Chapter along with the jet sizes, engine idle speed and the throttle needle setting for each model type.
2 If fuel starvation or persistent flooding of the carburettor is encountered, the float height should be checked. To allow this to be carried out the float chamber should be detached from the carburettor body and the fuel tap assembly and positioned as shown in the accompanying figure. The distance measured is between the carburettor body mating flange and the lower surface of the float and should be as listed in the Specifications at the beginning of this Chapter for the particular

pressed out from above by passing a wooden rod down through the throttle valve bore.
6 The choke assembly cannot be dismantled. If after careful cleaning, signs of wear or damage are found, the complete carburettor must be renewed. Check carefully the butterfly valve spindle pivot points for wear, as well as the operating arm and return spring.
7 To remove the throttle stop and pilot mixture screws, screw in each one until it seats lightly and record the exact number of turns necessary to achieve this. On refitting, screw in each one until it seats lightly, then unscrew it by the previous recorded number of turns to return the carburettor to its original setting. This will provide a basis for subsequent adjustment.
8 Clean the carburettor components carefully, taking precautions to prevent the risk of fire if petrol is used as a cleaning agent. Use only compressed air to clean out jets and passages; a tyre pump can be used if a compressor is not available. As a last resort, a jet may be unblocked using a nylon bristle from a toothbrush; never use wire or a pin for this purpose as the jet will be damaged.
9 Renew all O-rings as a matter of course; all such components are supplied in a carburettor gasket kit.
10 Note that if excessive quantities of dirt or water are found in the carburettor, the fuel tank should be drained and flushed out.

Fig. 8.12 Measuring the float height

Fig. 8.13 Bend the tab on the float pivot to adjust the float height

8.1 Displace rubber cover to adjust choke friction control – Z-2 and Z-Z models

model type. The float height can be adjusted by carefully bending the tab on the float pivot against which the top of the float needle abuts.

8 Choke: adjustment, removal and refitting

1 Check the choke control for correct operating by moving the handlebar-mounted choke knob over its full range checking for smooth operation whilst doing so. If any indication of roughness or binding is apparent, check along the length of the operating cable for signs of damage to the cable outer and renew the cable if necessary. Ensure that any binding of the choke control is not caused by maladjustment of the friction control located beneath the rubber cover which itself is located beneath the choke knob (Z-2 and Z-Z models only). Remove the cover from the friction control and turn the control anti-clockwise to lessen the resistance placed upon the shaft passing through it. If, with the control fully loosened, binding of the choke control is still apparent, the cable must be suspect. The friction control should be adjusted so that the choke knob stays where it is positioned throughout its operating range but without any great effort being required to move it from that position.
2 To remove the choke control assembly from the machine, first disconnect the cable from the retaining clamp on the carburettor-mounted bracket by unscrewing the single crosshead retaining screw. Release the cable from the clamp located just above the ignition switch and push up on the carburettor-mounted choke lever to release the cable nipple from the lever end. Move to the choke knob assembly and unscrew the crosshead screw retaining the assembly mounting plate to the handlebar casing on all Z-2 and Z-Z models. With the screw removed, the complete choke control assembly together with the cable may be withdrawn through the handlebar casing. On all later models unscrew the choke lever pivot screw and remove the lever so that it can be disengaged from the cable end nipple. The cable can then be pulled clear of the handlebar casing.
3 To refit the choke control assembly, reverse the procedure given for removal whilst noting the following points. Ensure that the cable is correctly routed and does not follow any tight curves along its length. Before tightening the clamp retaining the cable outer to the carburettor-mounted bracket, push the choke knob fully in and check that the choke butterfly valve is fully open by pressing down on the end of the carburettor-mounted lever. On completion of the fitting procedure, carry out the adjustment procedure given in paragraph 1.

8.2a Remove single retaining screw ...

8.2b ... to withdraw choke cable assembly – Z-2 and Z-Z models

8.2c Remove pivot screw and withdraw lever to release choke cable – later models

8.3 Ensure choke cable is routed correctly through clamps provided

9 Air filter: removal and refitting – C50/70-C, E models and C90-C, E, G, N, P, T, M-F, M-G, M-N, M-P, M-T models

1 A modified type of air filter is fitted to these models which must be removed for cleaning every 1500 miles. Although it is not strictly necessary to remove the legshields to gain access to the filter, work is a great deal easier if this is done.
2 Remove the four screws securing the two halves of the filter casing, then slacken the air filter hose clamp screw and disconnect the hose from the carburettor. Turn the forks to full lock (either side) and carefully manoeuvre the casing lower half away from the machine.
3 The element can then be detached from the casing half and cleaned or renewed, as necessary, as described in Routine Maintenance.

10 CDI ignition system: description and fault diagnosis – C50/70-C, E models and C90-C, E, G, N, P, T, M-F, M-G, M-N, M-P, M-T models

1 These models are fitted with an electronic ignition system which requires no maintenance other than to the spark plug and has no provision for adjustment.
2 The system is powered by a source coil built into the generator stator and is triggered by a pulser coil which is also mounted on the stator plate, but outside the rotor, to align with a magnetic trigger set in the rotor rim. The heart of the system is the CDI unit which is mounted next to the battery, behind the right-hand side cover; the only other component in the system, apart from the ignition switch and related wiring, is the HT coil which is mounted as described in Section 11.
3 If a fault should occur it can be traced by eliminating the components of the system in a logical order. This is as follows:

a) *Faulty spark plug or suppresser cap*
b) *Loose, corroded or damaged wiring connections, broken or shorted wiring between any of the system components*
c) *Faulty ignition switch*
d) *Faulty HT coil*
e) *Faulty CDI unit*
f) *Faulty generator coils*

4 The first three items can be checked as described in Chapters 4 and 7; refer to the subsequent Sections of this Chapter for details of testing the remaining components.
5 On C90-E and later models an intermittent ignition switch

9.2a Air filter removal (later models) – slacken air filter hose clamp screw ...

9.2b ... and remove four screws to release filter casing lower half

9.3 Pull element off casing half for cleaning and/or renewal

11.2a Ignition coil removal (C90M models) remove battery tray ...

11.2b ... detach starter relay and unbolt regulator/rectifier unit bracket ...

11.2c ... and inner mounting bracket – note CDI unit (arrowed) and flashing indicator relay

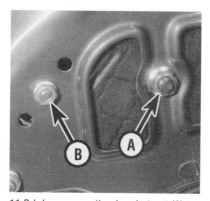

11.2d Inner mounting bracket nut (A) and ignition HT coil nut (B) on frame left-hand side

11.3 Ignition HT coil is removed through aperture in frame right-hand side

1 Duct
2 Casing top half
3 Seal
4 Bolt – 2 off
5 Spacer – 2 off
6 Grommet
7 Element
8 Casing bottom half
9 Screw – 4 off
10 Carburettor hose
11 Clamp
12 Screw

Fig. 8.14 Air filter – C50/70-C, E models and C90-C, E, G, N, P, T, M-F, M-G, M-N, M-P, M-T models

fault could be due to melted or burnt-out terminal plates, caused by a short circuit between the IG (black/white wire) and E (green wire) terminals. If this is found to be the case a modified switch is available to cure the fault.

11 Ignition HT coil: locating and testing – C50/70C, E models and C90-C, E, G, N, P, T, M-F, M-G, M-N, M-P, M-T models

Location

1 The ignition coil is mounted inside of the frame section, beneath the fuel tank. Remove the right and left-hand side covers. Remove the battery.
2 On kickstart models (all models except the C90M), remove the battery inner holder; it is retained by a single bolt at the bottom and by a nut on the frame left-hand side. On electric start models (C90M) remove the battery tray (it is retained by two bolts) and release the forward bracket which mounts the regulator/rectifier unit and starter relay. Remove the inner components mounting bracket from inside the frame; it is retained by a single bolt at the bottom and a nut on the left-hand side of the frame. Being careful not to strain any of the wiring, manoeuvre the inner bracket out complete with CDI unit and flashing indicator relay.
3 On all models, reach inside the frame aperture to access the ignition coil, which is retained to the left-hand side of the frame by a single nut. Having released this nut from the left-hand side of the frame, pull the coil towards the opening and disconnect the low tension wires. Where the coil HT lead has a plastic nut retaining it to the coil this can be removed to allow the coil to be withdrawn, otherwise the suppresser cap must be unscrewed, the HT lead released from the clamp on the engine and the lead retracted beneath the frame.

PRIMARY

H 12625

SECONDARY

Fig. 8.15 Ignition HT coil windings text C50/70-C, E models and C90-C, E, G, N, M-F, M-G, M-N models

4 Refitting is a reverse of the removal procedure. Note that the locating tab (C90-P, T and C90M-P, M-T models) or locating dowels on all earlier models, must engage the hole(s) in the frame. When reconnecting the battery, always connect the negative lead last.

Testing

5 If a weak spark or difficult starting causes the performance of the coil to be suspect, it should be tested by a Honda Service Agent or an auto-electrical expert. They will have the necessary equipment to test the spark gap and performance of the coil under load. It is, however, possible on certain models to measure the resistance of the coil's primary and secondary windings and thus gain an indication of the coil's condition.

Note that resistance figures are not available for the C90-P, T and C90M-P, M-T models.

6 Remove the coil as described above. If the HT lead was removed during coil removal it must be screwed back in place, although the suppresser cap must be taken off. Check the primary windings by connecting the meter probes between the low tension terminal (black/yellow wire connection) and the coil mounting lug. The reading should be in the region of 0.2 – 0.3 ohms.

7 To measure the secondary winding resistance, connect the meter between the HT lead end and the coil mounting lug. A reading in the region of 3.4 – 4.2 K ohms should be obtained.

8 If the resistance checks are widely different from the expected values, have your findings confirmed by a Honda Service Agent before renewing the coil. If faulty, the coil must be renewed – repairs are not possible.

---

12   CDI unit: testing – C50/70-C, E models and C90-C, E, G, N, P, T, M-F, M-G, M-N, M-P, M-T models

---

1 The CDI unit takes the form of a sealed box mounted behind the right-hand side cover. In the event of a malfunction the unit may be tested in place. Honda advise against the use of any test meter other than the Sanwa Electric Tester (Honda part number 07308-0020000) or the Kowa Electric Tester (TH-5H), because they feel that the use of other devices may result in inaccurate readings.

2 Most owners will find that they either do not possess a multimeter, in which case they may prefer to have the unit checked by a Honda Service Agent, or own a meter which is not of the specified make or model. In the latter case, a good indication of the unit's condition can be gleaned in spite of inaccuracies in the readings. If necessary, the CDI unit can be taken to a Honda Service Agent or auto-electrical specialist for confirmation of its condition.

3 The test details are given in the accompanying illustration in the form of a table of meter probe connections with the expected reading in each instance. If an ordinary multimeter is used the resistance range may be determined by trial and error. The diagram illustrates the CDI unit connections referred to in the table. For owners not possessing a test meter the unit or the complete machine can be taken to a Honda Service Agent for testing.

4 If the CDI unit is found to be faulty as a result of these tests it must be renewed. No repairs are possible. It might be worthwhile trying to obtain a good second-hand unit from a motorcycle breaker, in view of the cost of a new part.

12.1 CDI unit is rubber-mounted behind right-hand side cover

13.1 Pulser coil is mounted on generator stator, outside rotor

13 Ignition source and pulser coil: testing – C50/70-C, E models and C90-C, E, G, N, P, T, M-F, M-G, M-N, M-P, M-T models

C50/70-C, E and C90-C, E, G, N, M-F, M-G, M-N models

1 The ignition system is powered by a source coil and triggered by a pulser coil, both of which are built into the generator stator plate mounted on the left-hand side crankcase. It follows that if the generator malfunctions, it will affect the operation of the ignition system, possibly without affecting the remainder of the electrical system. Six leads exit from the stator assembly. Of these identify the plain green, the black/red, and the blue/white wires.

2 Disconnect the wires at their connectors. Using a multimeter set on the ohms scale measure the resistances between the terminals of those wires. The values should be as shown below.

Black/red to green lead (source coil) 50 – 170 ohm
Blue/white to green lead (pulser coil) 150 – 170 ohm

If the readings obtained fall outside the limits given, the generator stator is faulty. Unfortunately this means that the complete flywheel generator must be renewed; individual generator components are not available as spare parts. A check should be made to ensure that the fault is not due to a broken or damaged wire which could be repaired easily. If no apparent fault is found, it must be assumed that the coil or coils which gave the wrong reading has indeed malfunctioned. In such a case it is advised that the generator assembly be taken to an authorised Honda Service Agent for confirmation of this before a new assembly is purchased, as this is likely to be very expensive. Once more, a search around the motorcycle breakers might reveal a good second-hand assembly.

3 Note that these results apply only to C70-C, E, and C90C, E, G, N models. No information is available for the C50 or C90M models, although it is reasonable to assume that similar results can be expected. If in doubt, take the machine to a Honda Service Agent for the system to be tested.

C90-P, T and C90M-P, M-T models

4 Like the above models, the ignition system is powered by a source built into the generator stator, and triggered by a pulser coil, mounted next to the generator stator assembly. Five leads exit from the stator assembly and join the main wiring loom at a 4-pin and single connector under the legshield. The black/red wire comes from the ignition source coil, and the blue/yellow wire from the pulser coil.

5 No details are available from Honda to enable a check of the coil resistance, and thus determine whether it is at fault.

14 Ignition timing: checking – C50/70-C, E models and C90-C, E, G, N, P, T, M-F, M-G, M-N, M-P, M-T models

1 Due to the nature of the ignition system it is not possible to adjust the ignition timing in any way. Routine checks of the ignition timing therefore are not necessary, and should only be carried out when tracing the cause of a drop in performance. It must be stressed however that the ignition timing can only be checked; if it is found to be incorrect the generator rotor, stator or the CDI unit must be renewed.

2 The ignition timing can be checked only whilst the engine is running using a stroboscopic lamp and thus a suitable timing lamp will be required. The inexpensive neon lamps should be adequate in theory, but in practice may produce a pulse of such low intensity that the timing mark remains indistinct. If possible, one of the more precise xenon tube lamps should be employed, powered by an external source of the appropriate voltage.

3 On C90M models, unscrew the smaller inspection cap from the left-hand cover; on all other models, remove the complete cover. Connect the timing lamp to the machine as directed by the lamp's manufacturer. Start the engine and aim the lamp at the generator rotor. At idle speed (1700 rpm) the rotor 'F' mark should align exactly with the fixed index mark formed by a notch in the crankcase wall or cover aperture. Increase the engine speed to approximately 3000 rpm and check that the rotor full advance mark (two parallel lines) is now aligned with the fixed index mark.

4 In the event of the owner not having a tachometer with which to measure accurately the engine speed, the following method can be used, but must be regarded as only a rough guide. Start the engine and allow it to idle. Aim the timing lamp at the generator rotor. The fixed index mark should be approximately in the region of the 'F' mark. Slowly increase the engine speed. If the timing is correct, the full advance mark will appear to move round to line itself up with the fixed index mark, and it will then remain reasonably steady at that point regardless of engine speed. It will be realised that this is not an accurate method of checking the ignition timing and should only be regarded as a rough indication until the machine can be taken to an authorised Honda Service Agent. He should be able to check the ignition timing accurately, using a test unit fitted with a separate tachometer.

5 If there is any doubt about the ignition timing as a result of this check, take the machine to an authorised Honda Service Agent for an expert opinion. As already stated, there is no means of adjustment of the ignition timing on these machines, and renewal of the generator stator and rotor is the only solution to any fault. This is likely to prove rather expensive and an expert opinion should be sought to avoid wasting money.

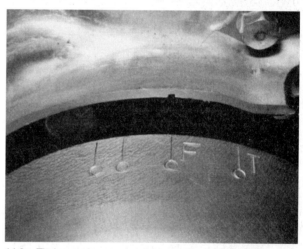

14.3a Timing marks on rotor rim must align with notch in crankcase wall as described in text

14.3b On C90M models, withdraw smaller inspection cap – timing marks must align as shown

15 Cycle parts: modifications

Handlebars, forks and steering head – removal and refitting

1 On C50/70-E models and C90-E, G, N, P, T, M-F, M-G, M-N, M-P, M-T models, a revised handlebar and steering head assembly is fitted. Refer to the following section for details.

Front forks – modification

2 The C90-G, N, P, T, M-G, M-N, M-P, M-T models do not have grease nipples in the front fork bottom link assemblies as on previous models. Accordingly, routine greasing of the assembly cannot be carried out as described in the Routine maintenance section of this manual.

3 The new assembly features parallel-sided bushes which are sealed by O-rings on each side to retain the grease. Re-greasing should not be required as often as with the previous type, but if stiffness of the assembly is noted, it must be dismantled and packed with fresh grease. Refer to Chapter 5, Section 3 for overhaul details.

Seat – removal and refitting

4 The seat pivots at the front end and can be removed either by unscrewing the two mounting nuts which secure it to the upper part of the hinge, or by unscrewing the two bolts which secure the hinge lower half (and the front of the fuel tank) to the frame.

Pillion footrests

5 On all models except the C50Z-A (C50L) model, the pillion footrests pivot on a single clevis pin which is secured by a split-pin and washer.

Rear suspension units

6 The rear suspension units fitted to later models differ from the previous type in that the lower mounting eye is unscrewed to enable spring removal. Pull the spring bottom cover up to compress the spring and expose the locknut.

7 On reassembly, note that the spring's closer-pitched coils must be uppermost and that thread locking compound should be applied to the damper rod threads before refitting the locknut and the bottom mounting eye. Screw the eye as far as possible onto the damper rod, then tighten the locknut securely. On C50Z-Z and C50Z-A (C50L) models note that the suspension unit bottom mountings are inboard of the swinging arm brackets, with the cap nuts on the outside.

Side stand

8 On C50/70-E models and C90-E, G, N, P, T, M-F, M-G, M-N, M-P, M-T models, the side stand is equipped with a rubber block on its end. This is intended as a safety device, designed to flip the stand up in the event of the rider forgetting to retract it before moving off. The block must be renewed when it wears down to the wear limit line.

Front and rear wheel – removal and refitting

9 A plain self-locking nut is used on C90-P, T and M-P, M-T models instead of the castellated nut and split pin fitted to all previous models.

---

16 Handlebar, forks and steering head: removal and refitting – C50/70-E models and C90-E, G, N, P, T, M-F, M-G, M-N, M-P, M-T models

---

Handlebar

1 Slacken and remove the two headlamp securing screws and disengage the headlamp from the handlebar nacelle. Disconnect the headlamp and parking lamp wiring and place the headlamp on one side. Wrap tape around the top of the speedometer cable to prevent the knurled ring slipping down the cable once released, then disconnect the cable from the speedometer. Trace the speedometer wiring back to the connectors and disconnect it. The speedometer can be removed after squeezing together the locating clips on each

H.16937

4	Screw – 2 off
5	Screw – 2 off
6	Nut – 2 off
7	Screw – 2 off
8	Screw – 2 off
9	Handlebar bracket top half
10	Steering stem nut
11	Washer
12	Bolt – 2 off
13	Washer – 2 off
14	Rubber seat
15	Spacer
16	Spacer – 2 off
17	Top bridge
18	Bolt – 5 off
19	Washer
20	Rubber seat
21	Top plate

1	Handlebar
2	Bolt – 2 off
3	Headlamp nacelle

Fig. 8.16 Handlebar and steering top bridge assembly –
C50/70-E models and C90-E, G, N, P, T, M-F, M-G, M-N, M-P, M-T models

16.1a Remove the headlamp unit to gain access inside the nacelle

16.1b Unscrew the knurled ring to free the speedometer cable

16.2a Remove the two screws (arrowed) on each side of the nacelle lower section ...

16.2b ... followed by the screw and nut on each side of the headlamp recess ...

16.2c ... and the single screw at the rear of the nacelle

16.2d The upper section of the nacelle can now be lifted away

16.3a Remove the flashing indicator lamps (two screws)

16.3b Disconnect the choke cable outer at the handlebar end, then disengage the nipple from the lever

16.4 Remove pivot bolt (A) and free brake lever. Remove screws (B) to free switch halves

16.5 Release the two bolts and the single screw to free handlebar

16.10a Remove the two bolts (A) to gain access to slotted nut (B)

16.10b Improvised modification to socket allows slotted nut to be removed (see text)

side of the instrument casing. Lift the speedometer out from the top of the nacelle.

2 Remove, from the underside of the nacelle, the four screws (two on each side) which secure the lower half of the nacelle to the upper half. Working through the headlamp opening, remove the two nacelle front securing screws and their nuts on the inner edge; take care not to let the nuts fall down into the fork assembly. Working through the top opening, remove the single rear screw. The upper half of the nacelle can now be lifted free.

3 Disconnect the various wiring connectors inside the nacelle area. Remove the flashing indicator lamps, each of which is retained by two screws. Release the choke cable clamp by removing its retaining screw, then disengage the choke cable from the lever. Remove the two screws which retain the halves of the left-hand handlebar switch unit and pull it clear of the handlebar.

4 Slide back the front brake lever dust cover, remove the pivot screw and disengage the lever. Unhook the cable from the lever. Separate the halves of the right-hand switch unit. Unhook the throttle cable and remove the twistgrip from the handlebar end.

5 Release the two handlebar mounting bolts and the single screw, then lift the handlebar off the steering head. Remove the nacelle lower half. Remove the single screw which retains the steering column front cover and lift it away. Remove the three handlebar bracket bolts and remove the bracket.

6 Refitting is a reverse of the removal procedure, noting the following points.

7 Tighten the handlebar bracket bolts to 2.0 – 2.5 kgf m (14 – 18 lbf ft). Tighten the handlebar mounting bolts to 2.0 – 3.0 kgf m (14 – 22 lbf ft). When fitting the throttle twistgrip, apply grease to the pulley section. Align the joint of the switch halves with the punch mark on the handlebar. Remember to check and adjust the throttle cable and front brake cable and to check the operation of all controls before riding the machine.

Forks and steering head

8 Remove the handlebar and handlebar bracket as described above.

9 Ensure that the machine is securely supported on its stand, with blocks placed under the crankcase to prevent it toppling when the front end is removed. Remove the front wheel (see Chapter 6).

10 Remove the two bolts which pass down through the top bridge assembly, leaving access clear to the steering stem nut. To remove this nut, a Honda locknut wrench and an extension bar are required. Alternatively, use the improvised method shown in the accompanying photograph and line drawing to adapt a normal socket for this purpose. Slacken and remove the nut, then lift off the top bridge washer, the rubber seat below it, and the three spacers. Remove the top bridge, followed by the washer and rubber seat. Release the two bolts which retain the fork top plate to the front fork assembly, then lift this away to reveal the steering stem and adjuster nut.

11 Support the fork assembly, then slacken and remove the bearing adjuster nut. The fork assembly can now be lowered clear of the steering head, taking care not to lose any of the steering head balls if they drop free. Lift off the top bearing cone.

12 Clean and examine the bearings and races prior to reassembly.

13 Coat the steering head bearing balls and bearing cups in heavy grease. The grease will hold the balls in the cups whilst the fork assembly is refitted. Carefully insert the steering stem through the bearing races, taking care not to dislodge the balls. Place the top cone in position, then fit the adjuster nut finger-tight to secure the assembly.

14 Tighten the locknut to take up bearing freeplay, moving it only a fraction of a turn at a time. **Caution:** *Never overtighten, otherwise there is a danger of placing too high a loading on the bearings and causing their premature failure. Note that the object of this adjustment is to remove all play from the steering head bearings, yet at the same time allowing the fork assembly to move freely from side to side.*

15 Continue reassembly in the reverse of the dismantling sequence, noting that the steering stem nut should be tightened to 6.0 – 9.0 kgf m (43 – 65 lbf ft). Refit the two top bridge bolts and tighten them to 2.0 – 2.5 kgf m (14 – 18 lbf ft). Refit the handlebar and bracket and handlebar as described above.

Fig. 8.17 Improvised method for releasing the steering stem nut

(–)Probe (+)Probe	S W	EXT	PC	E	IGN
SW		∞	∞	∞	∞
EXT	0.1–10		∞	∞	* ∞
PC	0.5–200	0.5–50		0.1–50	∞
E	0.2–30	0.1–10	∞		∞
IGN	∞	∞	∞	∞	

MEASURING RANGE(SANWA TESTER) x KΩ
MEASURING RANGE (KOWA TESTER) x 100Ω
* Needle swings and then returns to ∞

Fig. 8.18 Testing the CDI unit – C50/70-C, E models and C90-C, E, G, N, P, T, M-F, M-G, M-N, M-P, M-T models

17 Brake wear indicators: general

1 Later models are equipped with wear indicators on both brakes to provide an easy check of the amount of friction material remaining without having to remove the wheels.
2 When the brake is correctly adjusted, as described in Routine Maintenance, and is fully applied, the arrow on the pointer attached to the brake camshaft should not align with or move beyond the arrow mark cast on the brake backplate if the brake shoes are still in serviceable condition. If the pointer aligns with the cast mark or moves beyond it the wheel must be removed from the machine and the brake dismantled for examination.
3 If the friction material of either brake shoe is worn at any point to a thickness of 2.0 mm (0.08 in) or less, both brake shoes must be renewed, as described in Chapter 6. On reassembly, note that the wear indicator pointer can only be fitted the correct way to the brake camshafts as a wider spline on the inside of the pointer must engage the groove in the camshaft splines.

17.1 External indicators fitted to later models permit brake wear to be checked without dismantling wheels

18 Electrical system: general – C50/70-C, E models and C90-C, E, G, N, P, T, M-F, M-G, M-N, M-P, M-T models

1 All later models are fitted with a 12 volt electrical system powered by an AC generator mounted on the crankshaft left-hand end. Output is controlled by a combined regulator/rectifier unit mounted next to the battery, behind the right-hand side cover. On all C models a separate resistor is fitted immediately above the cylinder barrel to soak up excess current generated when the lighting switch is in the 'P' position; this is not fitted to later models which employ a more sophisticated regulator/rectifier unit.
2 Apart from the specific components described in the subsequent Sections of this Chapter the electrical system remains essentially the same as that described in Chapter 7. Note that all switches can be tested using an ohmmeter or multimeter to check that continuity exists only where indicated in the relevant parts of the wiring diagrams at the back of this Manual.
3 Since a switch can only be renewed if it is found to be faulty, there is nothing to be lost by attempting to dismantle it and to repair the fault. For example it may be possible to build up worn contacts with solder or to clean them with fine emery paper if they are dirty; if the fault is due to a broken or trapped wire this can usually be repaired easily by the owner. Switch life can be prolonged by regular spraying with WD40 or a similar water-dispersant lubricant.
4 Note that a battery's normal charging rate is 1/10th of its capacity; therefore the 4Ah batteries fitted to most later models, for example, should be charged at 0.4 amps. A higher charging rate should be used only in an emergency, as described in Chapter 7.

an ammeter between the battery positive terminal and its positive lead. On all C models disconnect the white/black wire at the regulator/rectifier unit block connector; on all other models disconnect the green wire at the regulator/rectifier unit block connector.
3 Check that the lights are switched off and start the engine. Charging should start (ie reach a reading of 13.4 volts at least) at 1500 rpm. Increase engine speed as shown below, when the following readings should be obtained:

@ 4000 rpm 15.8V/at least 1.0 A
@ 8000 rpm 16.6V/3.0 A maximum

4 Repeat the test with the lights switched on and the headlamp in the dip position. Charging should start at least at 1200 rpm and the following readings should be obtained:

@ 4000 rpm 16.9V/at least 1.5 A
@ 8000 rpm 17.4V/4.5 A maximum

5 If the results obtained differ significantly from those obtained, the components of the charging system must be checked individually, as described in subsequent Sections of this Chapter, until the fault is traced and eliminated.
6 Note however that if the battery is repeatedly found to be discharged it may be due to excessive use of the flashing indicators, horn, stop lamp and other electrical circuits, thus placing too heavy a demand on a system which is otherwise in perfect working order. This is usually found in the winter months and can be cured only be removing the battery at regular intervals to give it refresher charges.

19 Charging system: checking the output C50/70-C, E models and C90-C, E, G, N, P, T, M-F, M-G, M-N, M-P, M-T models

Note: *The C90M-F, M-G, M-N, M-P, M-T and C90-P, T models are fitted with a different type of generator for which no test data is available. Seek the advice of a Honda Service Agent if a charging system fault is suspected.*

1 The battery must be fully charged and in good condition for the test results to be accurate.
2 Start the engine and allow it to warm up to normal operating temperature then stop it and remove the right-hand side cover to expose the battery. Disconnect the battery positive (+) lead, then connect a DC voltmeter across the battery terminals and

20 Flywheel generator charging coil(s): testing – C50/70-C, E models and C90-C, E, G, N, P, T, M-F, M-G, M-N, M-P, M-T models

Testing

1 The charging and lighting systems on C50/70-C, E and C90-C, E, G, N, M-F, M-G, M-N models are powered by a single generator coil. On C90-P, T and M-P, M-T models, five of the stator plate coils power the charging and lighting systems, the sixth is the ignition source coil.
2 The following test can be made to determine the coil condition on C50/70-C, E and C90-C, E, G, N models. No test details are available for other models. Remove the legshield and trace the generator wires up to the block connector. Separate the connector and measure the resistance between

the white and green wire terminals on the generator side of the connector – a reading of 0.3 to 0.6 ohm should be obtained. Next measure the resistance between the yellow and green leads – a reading of 0.2 to 0.6 ohm should be obtained. If the readings are wildly different from these values the coil is faulty and should be renewed, although note that infinitely high resistance may be due to a broken wire connection or poor joint at the coil.

Coil removal and refitting – C50/70-C, E and C90-C, E, G, N, P, T models

3 Remove the legshield and disconnect the wiring from the generator at the block connector.
4 Remove the gear lever pinch bolt and pull it off its shaft. Remove the engine left-hand cover and free the neutral switch wire from the end of the switch.
5 The generator rotor must be removed to access the coil(s). Lock the engine and remove the nut and washer from the crankshaft left-hand end. Thread the Honda generator removal tool (Part No. 07733-0010000) into the rotor and tighten down its centre bolt to draw the rotor off the crankshaft taper.
6 On C50/70-C, E and C90-C, E, G, N models, the charging coil (identified by its white and yellow wires) can be unscrewed from the stator plate, although check first whether it can be purchased separately from the stator plate. If not, place a container underneath the crankcase to catch any oil loss and remove the two screws to free the generator stator from the crankcase. Note the large O-ring around the stator periphery and the O-rings on the stator plate screws; these should be renewed on reassembly. Top up the engine oil afterwards.
7 On the C90-P, T models, remove the two generator coil bolts and the two pulser coil bolts to free the coil assembly.

Coil removal and refitting – C90M models

8 Remove the legshield and disconnect the wiring from the generator at the block connector.
9 Remove the gear lever pinch bolt and pull it off its shaft. Remove the engine left-hand cover and the sprocket cover. Free the neutral switch wire from the end of the switch.
10 The generator stator coil(s) are contained inside the engine left-hand cover. Remove the wiring clamp bolt, the two bolts retaining the stator plate to the casing, and on M-P and M-T models only, the two bolts retaining the remote ignition pulser coil.

20.10 Charging coils (A), pulser coil (B) and wiring clamp (C) on C90M-P, M-T models

21.1 Regulator/rectifier unit – later models

21 Regulator/rectifier unit: testing – C50/70-C, E models and C90-C, E, G, N, P, T, M-F, M-G, M-N, M-P, M-T models

1 The regulator/rectifier unit is a sealed, heavily-finned unit mounted next to the battery, behind the right-hand side cover. To remove the unit disconnect the wires by pulling away the multi-pin block connector and unscrew the single mounting bolt.
2 To test the unit, Honda recommend the use either of a Sanwa SP-10D electrical tester set to the kilo ohms range, or of a Kowa TH-5H tester set to the x 100 ohms range. Ordinary ohmmeters or multimeters may be used but may give slightly different readings; the resistance range to be used must be determined by trial and error. If the correct equipment is not used, the test should be regarded as only a guide to the unit's condition and should be confirmed by a Honda Service Agent before any firm conclusions are drawn.
3 The test details are given in the accompanying charts; ensure that the correct chart is followed for the machine being tested. The charts take the form of meter probe connections with the expected reading in each instance.
4 If the results obtained differ markedly at any point from those given, the unit is faulty and must be renewed as repairs are not possible.

22 Resistor: testing – C models

1 The resistor is mounted as described in Section 18 of this Chapter and is easily identified by the single pink wire leading to it. It requires no maintenance other than to ensure that its mounting bolt is tight and that its mating surfaces are clean and dry so that a good earth connection is present. It will be necessary to remove the legshields to reach it.
2 If symptoms arise such as constantly blowing bulbs which appear to indicate a resistor fault, the unit can be tested by disconnecting the pink wire and measuring the resistance between the unit's wire terminal and a good earth point on the engine or frame.
3 A reading of 6.7 ohms should be obtained; if the reading measured is significantly above or below this figure, the resistor is faulty and must be renewed.

23 Fuel gauge circuit: testing – C50/70-E models and C90-E, G, N, P, T, M-F, M-G, M-N, M-P, M-T models

1 The fuel gauge circuit comprises a float-type sender unit which incorporates a variable resistance and is mounted in the fuel tank. The gauge unit is mounted in the speedometer head.
2 The gauge is removed and refitted with the speedometer assembly; see Section 16 of this Chapter. On C50/70/90-E and C90M-F models the gauge is part of the speedometer and must be renewed with it. On C90-G, N, P, T and M-G, M-N, M-P, M-T models remove the retaining screws and lift off the speedometer top cover, disconnect the electrical leads by removing the terminal screws and withdraw the gauge unit which is secured to the speedometer assembly by small screws.
3 On all models, the sender unit can be removed from the tank by unscrewing its four retaining screws and lifting it out, take care not to damage or bend the float. Renew the sealing gasket prior to refitting to prevent the possibility of leaks.
4 To test the system, first ensure that the battery is fully charged by checking that all other electrical circuits function normally. If a fully-charged battery does not cure the fault, disconnect the sender unit at its two-pin block connector and bridge, with a spare length of wire, the two terminals of the wires leading into the main loom. Switch on the ignition. The gauge needle should immediately swing over to the 'Full' mark. Disconnect the two wires, whereupon the needle should swing back to the 'Empty' mark. Switch off the ignition. Carry out this check as quickly as possible or the gauge unit may be damaged.
5 If the gauge needle moves as described, it can be assumed that it is in good order and that the fault lies in the sender unit. If the needle does not move properly, the fault must lie in the gauge unit or in the wiring between the two. Check the wires carefully for faults before going to the expense of renewing the gauge/speedometer unit.
6 To test conclusively the sender unit, remove it from the tank and connect a multimeter across its wire terminals. With the float raised to the 'Full' position or 32.5 mm (1.28 in) below a horizontal line extending from the unit mounting flange (ie below the fuel tank top surface) a resistance of 4 – 10 ohms should be measured. In the 'Reserve' position (111.0 mm/4.37 in below the mounting flange) the reading should increase to 66 – 75 ohms. In the 'Empty' position (float fully depressed, or 123.5 mm/4.86 in) the reading should be 90 – 100 ohms.
7 If it is found to be faulty, the sender unit must be renewed; repairs are not possible.

24 Charging rate: boosting – C50/70Z-2, Z-Z models

1 These machines' electrical systems can be modified to boost the charging rate if the need arises. If the machine is used mainly at night, or at low speeds with extensive use of the flashing indicators and stop lamp, or if it is used infrequently, the standard electrical system may not be able to keep pace with the demand placed on it, with the result that the battery is repeatedly in a low state of charge or even goes flat.
2 Remove the right-hand side cover to expose the battery. On C50/70Z-2 models disconnect the green/red wire from the pink-banded green/red wire and connect it to the pink wire instead. On C50/70Z-Z models disconnect the pink-banded white/black wire from the pink wire and connect it to the white/black wire instead.
3 **Warning:** This modification will produce an increased charging rate which is suitable only for short trips or low-speed work. If the machine is used on a long journey or at high speed, the charging system must be converted back to the standard connections or the battery will be over-charged. If this is allowed to happen, excessive quantities of electrolyte will be lost through evaporation and the battery may be severely damaged.

23.1a Fuel gauge unit is mounted in speedometer head

23.1b Fuel gauge sender unit is mounted in fuel tank top surface

– \ +	W	R	W/Bl
W		1-20	∞
R	∞		∞
W/Bl	∞	∞	

C50, 70, 90-C models

– \ +	W	R	Y	G
W		0.5-10	∞	∞
R	∞		∞	∞
Y	∞	∞		1-5
G	∞	∞	1-5	

C70-E models
C50-E models up to frame no. 9039834
C90-E models up to frame no. 1339498

– \ +	W	R	Y	G
W		0.5-10*	∞	∞
R	∞		∞	∞
Y	∞	∞		5-100
G	∞	∞	5-100	

C50-E models from frame no 9039835
C90-E models from frame no 1339499
C90-G, N, M-F, M-G, M-N models

*3 – 50 for C90 models from frame no. 1428388

Fig. 8.19 Testing the regulator/rectifier unit

(test tables for C90-P, T and M-P, M-T models are not available)

25.2 Peel back rubber cover and disconnect starter motor lead

25.4 Disconnect all generator lead wires to release engine left-hand cover

4 Note that the modification should only be made after the system has been thoroughly checked and found to be in good condition. In normal usage the charging system will be completely adequate and should not require modification unless the machine is used under the severe conditions described in paragraph 1 of this Section.

25 Starter motor: removal and refitting – C90M-F, M-G, M-N, M-P, M-T models

1 Remove the right-hand side cover, disconnect the battery (negative terminal first), and remove the legshield.
2 Pull back the rubber cover, remove the retaining screw and disconnect the lead from the starter motor.
3 Remove its retaining bolts and withdraw the gearbox sprocket cover.
4 Disconnect the generator lead wires at the connectors joining them to the main wiring loom, then disconnect the neutral indicator switch wire. Remove the gearchange lever, noting that its pinch bolt must be removed completely to permit this.
5 Remove its retaining bolts and withdraw the left-hand engine cover; a few taps using only a soft-faced mallet may be required to break the joint seal. Note the two locating dowels.

25.6a Withdraw retaining circlip from starter motor shaft ...

25.6b ... so that drive chain and sprocket can be removed

25.7 Unscrew mounting bolts (arrowed) to release starter motor

25.9a Fit new cover gasket over two locating dowels (arrowed) ...

25.9b ... and check generator coils are securely fastened inside cover before refitting

6 Withdraw the circlip from the starter motor shaft and pull the drive sprocket and chain off the shaft splines. Be careful not to allow the engine to rotate, or the chain may jam; ensure that the chain is kept secure at all times. Renew the circlip if it is distorted or damaged in any way.
7 Remove the three starter motor mounting bolts and withdraw the motor.
8 On refitting, renew the O-ring around the motor left-hand end and apply a thin smear of grease to it. Refit the motor and tighten securely its mounting bolts, then refit the sprocket and chain to the motor shaft, and secure the sprocket with its retaining circlip.
9 Check that the two locating dowels are in place in the crankcase mating surface and fit a new gasket over them. Check that the generator stator plate and coils are securely fastened to the inside of the engine left-hand cover, then refit the cover and tighten its retaining screws securely.
10 Connect the generator lead wires and neutral indicator switch wire, then refit the gearbox sprocket cover and gearchange lever. Connect the starter motor lead to the motor terminal, smear a small amount of acid-free grease or petroleum jelly (Vaseline) over it to prevent corrosion then refit the rubber cover.
11 Re-connect the battery and check the operation of the motor before refitting the legshield.

26.2a Remove four retaining screws ...

26.2b ... to release reduction gear housing from motor assembly

26.2c Withdraw reduction gear as a single unit

Fig. 8.20 Starter motor and drive train – C90M-F, M-G, M-N, M-P, M-T models

1 Gearbox sprocket cover	14 Bolt – 3 off	27 Drive chain	40 O-ring
2 Bolt – 2 off	15 Cable clamp	28 Driven sprocket	41 Reduction gear housing
3 Bolt	16 Nut	29 Retaining plate	42 Reduction gear
4 Left-hand engine cover	17 Washer	30 Screw	43 Gasket
5 Gasket	18 Rotor	31 Drive sprocket	44 Brush holder housing
6 Dowel – 2 off	19 Locating pin	32 Circlip	45 O-ring
7 Bolt – 2 off	20 Backing plate	33 Chain guide	46 Starter motor body
8 Bolt	21 Starter clutch body	34 Chain guide	47 Bolt – 3 off
9 Plug	22 Screw – 3 off	35 Oil seal	48 Screw – 4 off
10 O-ring	23 Roller – 3 off	36 Screw – 2 off	49 Starter motor lead
11 Timing inspection plug	24 Plunger – 3 off	37 Blanking plate	50 Screw and washer
12 O-ring	25 Spring – 3 off	38 O-ring	51 Brush – 2 off
13 Stator plate (M-F, M-G, M-N model type shown)	26 Oil seal	39 O-ring – 2 off	52 Spring – 2 off

26 Starter motor: overhaul – C90M-F, M-G, M-N, M-P, M-T models

1 Remove the starter motor from the machine. See Section 25.

2 Unscrew the four retaining screws and withdraw the reduction gear housing from the motor assembly left-hand end. Peel off the gasket and withdraw the reduction gear.

3 Hold the starter motor shaft splined left-hand end as securely as possible without damaging it and pull off the plated metal body. *Note that the pull of the motor magnets is very strong and it will be easy to damage the motor components, particularly the brushes, unless great care is taken.* Place the motor body in a clean plastic bag so that it cannot attract any metal particles that may be lying about.

4 Carefully withdraw the starter motor armature from the end cover, noting the presence of any thrust washers, then clean all components and lay them out for inspection. Note: only the brushes and springs are available separately; if any other part of the motor itself is worn or damaged the complete motor assembly must be renewed.

5 The brushes are the only items that require regular attention. Measure the length of each and renew both if either is worn to a length of 4 mm (0.16 in) or less, or if either is chipped, or otherwise damaged. Note that while the length of a new brush is given as 12 mm (0.47 in) by the manufacturer, those (unworn) fitted to the machine featured in the accompanying photographs were found to be only 7 mm (0.28 in) long.

6 Check that both brushes are free to move easily in their holders; use a sharp knife and fine abrasive paper as necessary to trim or polish away any moulding flash or raised burrs from the nylon brush holder. Both brushes should show equal, even and full contact with the commutator; if not either renew the brushes or the springs or check carefully the brush holder. Renew the springs if there is any doubt about their condition. Note that the brush holder must be withdrawn before the positive (+ve) brush terminal can be renewed.

7 Clean the commutator segments with methylated spirit and inspect each one for scoring or discoloration. If any pair of segments is discoloured, a shorted armature winding is indicated. The manufacturer supplies no information regarding skimming and re-cutting the armature in the event of serious scoring or burning, and so by implication suggests that a new armature (therefore a new motor assembly) is the only solution. It is suggested, however, that the advice of a vehicle electrical specialist is sought first; professional help may work out a lot cheaper.

8 Honda advise against cleaning the commutator segments with abrasive paper, presumably because of the risk of abrasive particles becoming embedded in the soft segments. It is suggested, therefore, that an ink eraser be used to burnish the segments and remove any surface oxide deposits before installing the brushes.

9 Using a multimeter set on the resistance scale, check the continuity between pairs of segments, noting that anything other than a very low resistance indicates a partially or completely open circuit. Next check the armature insulation by checking for continuity between the armature core and each segment. Anything other than infinite resistance indicates an internal failure.

10 Check all remaining components for signs of wear or damage. As previously noted worn or damaged items cannot be repaired, they can only be renewed; in many cases this means the renewal of the complete assembly. All seals and gaskets can be renewed separately, and it may be possible to obtain bearings, such as that fitted to the reduction gear, from a motor factor or bearing supplier.

11 On reassembly, apply a thin smear of high melting-point grease to the bearing surface in the motor body. Fit each brush and spring in their holders and check that each brush is free to slide quite freely. Ensure that used brushes are refitted in their original positions because they will have worn to the profile of the commutator. Hold both brushes fully back in their holders and carefully insert the armature, with any thrust washers correctly refitted, between them. Allow the brushes to be

26.3 Grip armature shaft firmly on removing motor body – magnets are very strong

26.4 Clean thoroughly all components and check for wear

26.5 Measuring brush length

26.6a Negative brush is released by removing retaining screw

26.6b To remove positive brush, remove both screws and withdraw brush holder ...

26.6c ... then rotate terminal blade to release brush from holder

26.9a Checking commutator segments

26.9b Checking armature windings

26.11a Fit brush components as shown and note method used ...

26.11b ... to retain brushes against spring pressure while refitting armature

26.12 Do not forget to renew seals, gaskets and O-rings

26.13 Ensure reduction gear housing gasket is correctly refitted

returned against the commutator and check that each one is making a proper contact.

12 Grip the armature firmly at its left-hand (splined) end, then refit the motor body taking care that the sealing O-ring, the armature and the brushes are not displaced. Check that the armature rotates easily and that the sealing O-ring is correctly refitted.

13 Fit a new gasket before refitting the reduction gear and its housing. Tighten the retaining screws securely before refitting the motor to the machine.

14 The operation of the motor can be checked using two thick pieces of insulated wire as jumper leads. Connect one wire between the battery positive terminal and the motor terminal, keeping it well away from the motor body. Connect the second jumper to the motor body, using a nut and bolt to attach it to one of the mounting lugs. Check that when the free end of the second jumper is touched on the battery negative terminal, the motor turns freely.

27 Starter motor drive: removal, examination and refitting – C90M-F, M-G, M-N, M-P, M-T models

1 Remove the starter motor from the machine. See Section 25.

2 Remove its single retaining screw and withdraw the starter clutch driven sprocket retaining plate.

3 To prevent crankshaft rotation while its retaining nut is unscrewed, the generator rotor must be held with a strap wrench; do not use any other form of locking tool (other than the correct Honda service tool) and take great care not to damage the raised ignition trigger set in the outside of the rotor. Remove the nut and its plain washer.

4 The rotor should be drawn off the crankshaft using only the correct Honda service tool (part number 07933-KG20000), which is screwed on the external thread machined around the rotor centre boss.

5 If the correct tool is not available the only alternative is to apply a three-legged puller which has claws large enough to spread the load as much as possible and yet thin enough to fit fully behind the rotor. Owners should note that the rotor may be a very tight fit and the only way of preventing any risk of damage is to take the machine to an authorised Honda dealer so that the rotor can be removed safely by an expert using the correct service tool. If a legged puller is used, be careful to obtain and fit a spacer (we found an old gudgeon pin of the required size) to prevent damage to the crankshaft threaded end; at the very least, refit the rotor retaining nut and screw it down flush with the crankshaft end.

27.2 Remove screw to release driven sprocket retaining plate

27.3 Use strap wrench to hold rotor – take care not to damage ignition trigger

27.5a Extractor of type shown may be used only if correct service tool is not available

27.5b Take great care not to damage rotor and use spacer as shown to protect crankshaft end

27.6a Check chain guides for wear – note marks on outside faces to ensure correct refitting

27.6b Check blanking plate oil seal whenever rotor assembly is removed

27.7a Withdraw driven sprocket from rear of clutch and check needle bearing for wear ...

6 Remove the rotor, driven sprocket and chain as a single unit. If they are worn or damaged, renew the starter chain guides that are set in recesses in the crankcase wall; they are a press fit in the casing. Note that the larger of the two has a figure '4' embossed on its outside (left-hand) face; ensure that it is correctly refitted.

7 To check whether the starter clutch is operating correctly, fit the driven sprocket to the rear of the clutch and rotor. When rotated in a clockwise direction, as viewed from the sprocket side, the clutch should lock immediately, allowing power to be transmitted from the sprocket to the crankshaft. When rotated anti-clockwise, the sprocket should be free to run smoothly. If the movement is unsatisfactory, remove the sprocket from the clutch. The sprocket boss should be smooth, scoring or damage to the surface indicates that the rollers are similarly marked, and require further inspection.

8 The rollers, springs and plungers may be removed for examination with the clutch still attached to the rear of the rotor. Using a small, flat-bladed screwdriver, carefully push each plunger back against its spring tension until the roller can be removed. Then remove the springs and plungers. Signs of wear will be obvious and will necessitate renewal of the worn or damaged parts.

27.7b ... also oil seal – check sprocket boss is smooth and unworn

27.8a Press back clutch plunger as shown to release each roller

27.8b Renew plungers and springs if worn or damaged

27.9 Use impact driver to remove or refit clutch body screws – stake to prevent slackening on refitting

27.10 Ensure plungers and springs are correctly installed on reassembly

27.12a Rotor, driven sprocket and chain must be removed and refitted as one unit

27.12b Tighten rotor nut to specified torque wrench setting

9 To dismantle the clutch further, the three countersunk, crosshead retaining screws must be removed. Using an impact driver, slacken and remove the three screws. The clutch body and the backing plate can now be removed from the rear of the rotor. Note the single locating dowel between the rear of the rotor and the clutch body. Examine the clutch body for wear in the form of elongation or scoring of the roller housings. If worn badly, the body must be renewed.

10 On reassembly, ensure the dowel pin is correctly located, and apply a small quantity of locking fluid to each of the three retaining screws. Retighten them fully using an impact driver. Reinstall the springs, plungers and the rollers using the same procedure as employed for their removal.

11 Inspect the drive and driven sprockets, looking for chipped, worn, broken or missing teeth. Examine the drive chain for damaged rollers or fractured links. Wear of an excessive nature is extremely unlikely on the sprockets or the chain, due to its fully enclosed situation and limited usage, but note that since there is no provision for lubrication, a regular soaking in chain lubricant will help to prolong its life.

12 On reassembly, note that the driven sprocket, the chain and the rotor must be assembled and fitted as a single unit. Tighten the retaining nut to its specified torque setting then refit the driven sprocket retaining plate and tighten its screw securely.

13 Refit the starter motor. See Section 25.

28 Starter circuit: testing – C90M-F, M-G, M-N, M-P, M-T models

1 The starter circuit components consist of the starter button in the handlebar right-hand switch cluster and the relay, which is rubber-mounted behind the right-hand side cover, next to the battery.

2 In the event of a failure of the starter circuit, always check first that the battery is in good condition and fully charged. The motor draws a very heavy current compared with the rest of the electrical system, and it is not uncommon for the battery to

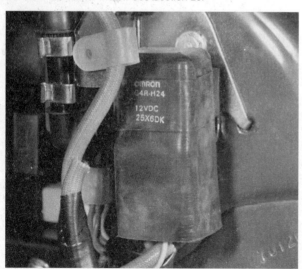

28.1 Starter relay is rubber-mounted next to battery

Fig. 8.21 Starter motor circuit diagram –
C90M-F, M-G, M-N, M-P, M-T models

become discharged just enough to prevent it from operating the starter successfully. If in doubt, remove the battery and recharge it as described in Section 18.

3 If the battery is fully charged and the starter still fails to operate, check the operation of the starter relay as described below then, if the fault persists, check the motor itself.

4 The starter relay acts as a remote switch, capable of switching the high current required by the starter motor. When the ignition is switched on and the starter button pressed, a small current is drawn by the relay windings as the main contacts are closed. These carry the high current drawn by the motor, and prevent arcing at the handlebar switch contacts. The operation of the relay can be checked using the machine's battery and a multimeter.

5 Unplug the relay wiring and remove it from its holder. Make up two insulated jumper leads, connecting one to the black lead terminal and its other end to the battery positive (+ve) terminal. Connect the second jumper lead to the yellow/red lead terminal of the unit, leaving its other end unconnected at present.

6 Connect a battery and bulb continuity tester or a multimeter set on the resistance (ohms) range between the red lead terminal and the red/white lead terminal. No continuity should be shown at this stage, but the circuit should be completed when the free end of the second jumper lead is touched on the battery negative (–ve) terminal. This should be accompanied by an audible click as the relay contacts close.

7 The above test should normally establish whether or not the relay is working. In rare cases the relay will work well enough to indicate a continuity reading, but the contacts may have become sufficiently burnt not to be able to cope with the heavy starter motor current. If this is the case it will be necessary to check by fitting a new unit.

8 The starter button is tested using a continuity tester or a multimeter to establish whether continuity exists between the switch wire terminals when the button is pressed. If not, the switch is faulty and must be renewed, although there is nothing to be lost in attempting a repair, by dismantling the switch and cleaning or repairing the contacts.

Wiring diagram – C50Z-2 and C70Z-2 models

Wiring diagram – C50Z-Z, C50Z-A (C50L) and C70Z-Z models

Wiring diagram – C90Z-2 and C90Z-Z models

Wiring diagram – C50-C, C70-C and C90-C models

Wiring diagram – C50-E, C70-E, C90-E, C90-G, C90-N, C90-P and C90-T models

Wiring diagram – C90M-F, C90M-G, C90M-N, C90M-P and C90M-T models

Conversion factors

Length (distance)

Inches (in)	x 25.4	= Millimetres (mm)	x 0.0394	= Inches (in)
Feet (ft)	x 0.305	= Metres (m)	x 3.281	= Feet (ft)
Miles	x 1.609	= Kilometres (km)	x 0.621	= Miles

Volume (capacity)

Cubic inches (cu in; in³)	x 16.387	= Cubic centimetres (cc; cm³)	x 0.061	= Cubic inches (cu in; in³)
Imperial pints (Imp pt)	x 0.568	= Litres (l)	x 1.76	= Imperial pints (Imp pt)
Imperial quarts (Imp qt)	x 1.137	= Litres (l)	x 0.88	= Imperial quarts (Imp qt)
Imperial quarts (Imp qt)	x 1.201	= US quarts (US qt)	x 0.833	= Imperial quarts (Imp qt)
US quarts (US qt)	x 0.946	= Litres (l)	x 1.057	= US quarts (US qt)
Imperial gallons (Imp gal)	x 4.546	= Litres (l)	x 0.22	= Imperial gallons (Imp gal)
Imperial gallons (Imp gal)	x 1.201	= US gallons (US gal)	x 0.833	= Imperial gallons (Imp gal)
US gallons (US gal)	x 3.785	= Litres (l)	x 0.264	= US gallons (US gal)

Mass (weight)

Ounces (oz)	x 28.35	= Grams (g)	x 0.035	= Ounces (oz)
Pounds (lb)	x 0.454	= Kilograms (kg)	x 2.205	= Pounds (lb)

Force

Ounces-force (ozf; oz)	x 0.278	= Newtons (N)	x 3.6	= Ounces-force (ozf; oz)
Pounds-force (lbf; lb)	x 4.448	= Newtons (N)	x 0.225	= Pounds-force (lbf; lb)
Newtons (N)	x 0.1	= Kilograms-force (kgf; kg)	x 9.81	= Newtons (N)

Pressure

Pounds-force per square inch (psi; lbf/in²; lb/in²)	x 0.070	= Kilograms-force per square centimetre (kgf/cm²; kg/cm²)	x 14.223	= Pounds-force per square inch (psi; lbf/in²; lb/in²)
Pounds-force per square inch (psi; lbf/in²; lb/in²)	x 0.068	= Atmospheres (atm)	x 14.696	= Pounds-force per square inch (psi; lbf/in²; lb/in²)
Pounds-force per square inch (psi; lbf/in²; lb/in²)	x 0.069	= Bars	x 14.5	= Pounds-force per square inch (psi; lbf/in²; lb/in²)
Pounds-force per square inch (psi; lbf/in²; lb/in²)	x 6.895	= Kilopascals (kPa)	x 0.145	= Pounds-force per square inch (psi; lbf/in²; lb/in²)
Kilopascals (kPa)	x 0.01	= Kilograms-force per square centimetre (kgf/cm²; kg/cm²)	x 98.1	= Kilopascals (kPa)
Millibar (mbar)	x 100	= Pascals (Pa)	x 0.01	= Millibar (mbar)
Millibar (mbar)	x 0.0145	= Pounds-force per square inch (psi; lbf/in²; lb/in²)	x 68.947	= Millibar (mbar)
Millibar (mbar)	x 0.75	= Millimetres of mercury (mmHg)	x 1.333	= Millibar (mbar)
Millibar (mbar)	x 0.401	= Inches of water (inH₂O)	x 2.491	= Millibar (mbar)
Millimetres of mercury (mmHg)	x 0.535	= Inches of water (inH₂O)	x 1.868	= Millimetres of mercury (mmHg)
Inches of water (inH₂O)	x 0.036	= Pounds-force per square inch (psi; lbf/in²; lb/in²)	x 27.68	= Inches of water (inH₂O)

Torque (moment of force)

Pounds-force inches (lbf in; lb in)	x 1.152	= Kilograms-force centimetre (kgf cm; kg cm)	x 0.868	= Pounds-force inches (lbf in; lb in)
Pounds-force inches (lbf in; lb in)	x 0.113	= Newton metres (Nm)	x 8.85	= Pounds-force inches (lbf in; lb in)
Pounds-force inches (lbf in; lb in)	x 0.083	= Pounds-force feet (lbf ft; lb ft)	x 12	= Pounds-force inches (lbf in; lb in)
Pounds-force feet (lbf ft; lb ft)	x 0.138	= Kilograms-force metres (kgf m; kg m)	x 7.233	= Pounds-force feet (lbf ft; lb ft)
Pounds-force feet (lbf ft; lb ft)	x 1.356	= Newton metres (Nm)	x 0.738	= Pounds-force feet (lbf ft; lb ft)
Newton metres (Nm)	x 0.102	= Kilograms-force metres (kgf m; kg m)	x 9.804	= Newton metres (Nm)

Power

Horsepower (hp)	x 745.7	= Watts (W)	x 0.0013	= Horsepower (hp)

Velocity (speed)

Miles per hour (miles/hr; mph)	x 1.609	= Kilometres per hour (km/hr; kph)	x 0.621	= Miles per hour (miles/hr; mph)

Fuel consumption*

Miles per gallon (mpg)	x 0.354	= Kilometres per litre (km/l)	x 2.825	= Miles per gallon (mpg)

Temperature

Degrees Fahrenheit = (°C x 1.8) + 32   Degrees Celsius (Degrees Centigrade; °C) = (°F - 32) x 0.56

It is common practice to convert from miles per gallon (mpg) to litres/100 kilometres (l/100km), where mpg x l/100 km = 282

English/American terminology

Because this book has been written in England, British English component names, phrases and spellings have been used throughout. American English usage is quite often different and whereas normally no confusion should occur, a list of equivalent terminology is given below.

English	American	English	American
Air filter	Air cleaner	Number plate	License plate
Alignment (headlamp)	Aim	Output or layshaft	Countershaft
Allen screw/key	Socket screw/wrench	Panniers	Side cases
Anticlockwise	Counterclockwise	Paraffin	Kerosene
Bottom/top gear	Low/high gear	Petrol	Gasoline
Bottom/top yoke	Bottom/top triple clamp	Petrol/fuel tank	Gas tank
Bush	Bushing	Pinking	Pinging
Carburettor	Carburetor	Rear suspension unit	Rear shock absorber
Catch	Latch	Rocker cover	Valve cover
Circlip	Snap ring	Selector	Shifter
Clutch drum	Clutch housing	Self-locking pliers	Vise-grips
Dip switch	Dimmer switch	Side or parking lamp	Parking or auxiliary light
Disulphide	Disulfide	Side or prop stand	Kick stand
Dynamo	DC generator	Silencer	Muffler
Earth	Ground	Spanner	Wrench
End float	End play	Split pin	Cotter pin
Engineer's blue	Machinist's dye	Stanchion	Tube
Exhaust pipe	Header	Sulphuric	Sulfuric
Fault diagnosis	Trouble shooting	Sump	Oil pan
Float chamber	Float bowl	Swinging arm	Swingarm
Footrest	Footpeg	Tab washer	Lock washer
Fuel/petrol tap	Petcock	Top box	Trunk
Gaiter	Boot	Torch	Flashlight
Gearbox	Transmission	Two/four stroke	Two/four cycle
Gearchange	Shift	Tyre	Tire
Gudgeon pin	Wrist/piston pin	Valve collar	Valve retainer
Indicator	Turn signal	Valve collets	Valve cotters
Inlet	Intake	Vice	Vise
Input shaft or mainshaft	Mainshaft	Wheel spindle	Axle
Kickstart	Kickstarter	White spirit	Stoddard solvent
Lower leg	Slider	Windscreen	Windshield
Mudguard	Fender		

Index